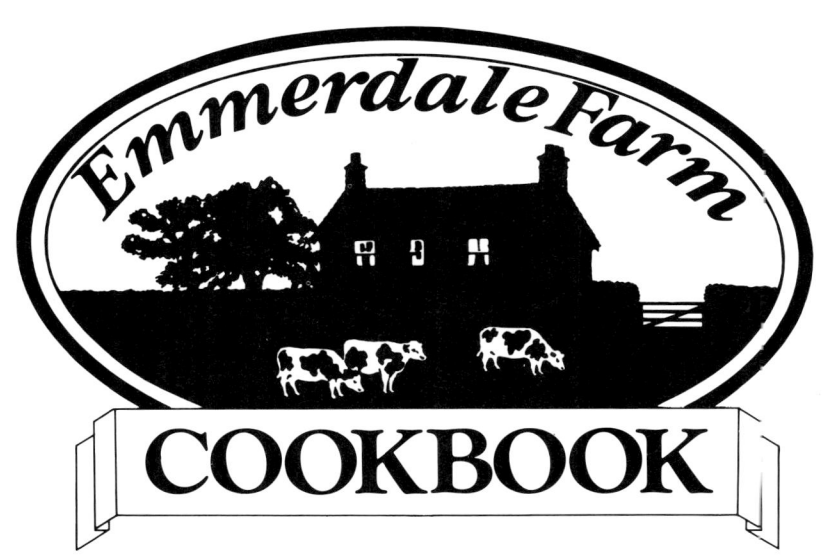

COOKBOOK

WARD LOCK LIMITED · LONDON

Acknowledgements

The publishers would like to thank the following organizations and companies for their help with the photographs in this book:

Anchor Foods Limited
Apple and Pear Development Council
British Sausage Bureau
Dairy Produce Advisory Service of The Milk Marketing Board
Eggs Information Bureau
Flour Advisory Bureau
Fresh Fruit and Vegetable Information Bureau
Guernsey Tomato Information Bureau
John West Foods Ltd
Kraft Foods Ltd
Mushroom Growers Association
New Zealand Lamb Information Bureau
Potato Marketing Board
RHM Foods Ltd
Seafish Industry Authority
Tate and Lyle Refineries
The Sugar Bureau

Photographs of location and cast supplied by Yorkshire Television Stills Department

Text copyright © Ward Lock Limited 1984
Emmerdale Farm copyright © Yorkshire Television Limited 1984

First published in Great Britain in 1984
by Ward Lock Limited, 82 Gower Street,
London WC1E 6EQ, a Pentos Company.

Layout by Niki Penn
Text set in Baskerville
by M & R Computerised Typesetting Ltd. Grimsby, England

Printed and bound in Spain by
Graficromo, S.A., Cordoba

British Library Cataloguing in Publication Data

The Emmerdale Farm cookbook.
1. Cookery, British
641.5941   TX717

ISBN 0–7063–6311–6

Contents

NOTES

It is important to follow *either* the metric *or* the imperial measures when using this book. Do *not* use a combination of measures.

Introduction

I've seen a great many changes in the Yorkshire Dales since I was a girl. Fifty years ago it was a very different place: I well remember the days when, come haymaking, the whole family would be summoned out to the fields, turning the hay with rakes after the scythemen had cut it. No-one had a tractor then in our part of the world; and when you wouldn't see a car from one week to the next it was a quieter place. We kept the old shorthorns in the dairy herd then, and some Highland cattle for beef. They were beautiful beasts, with their long, shaggy, golden coats. You don't see them very often in the Dales now the Friesians have caught on so much. Things are more mechanized now, I suppose. I will say it's made life a lot easier than it used to be—and if a Dales farmer would agree with me, I know his wife would too, because fifty years ago in the farmhouse kitchen the work never seemed to stop. I think back to what our kitchen used to look like when I was a young girl: the great hearth that warmed and fed us all, with its kail pot and trivet, the kettles and pans hanging from the reckan crook, kept polished till you could see your face in it. There were covered cheese-presses standing in a corner, oatcakes and griddlecakes drying on the breadflake above the oven, joints of pickled beef or sides of bacon hanging in the beef-loft. The old kitchen range with a roaring fire in the winter: it makes a pretty picture to think about, but it all meant a lot of hard work for the women. I still remember my mother tramping across the field to the farmhouse with a back can full of milk for butter and cheese-making: sometimes in the winter months we'd be working for hours in the dairy trying to make the butter come. We'd make cheese from May to October when there was good grazing, and the cheeses were all different, depending on the time of the year: grass cheese, pasture cheese, fog cheese, hay cheese; the pasture cheese was my favourite—that was the kind we'd make to go blue, and we'd save it for Christmas to eat with home-made biscuits, pickled walnuts, and port, if we could get it. Each season had its

different work, and it was after Harvest that was the busiest time, preserving fruit and vegetables from the garden, making jam, and, a little later in the year, preparing the meat. The men would kill the animals and we'd salt them, in a brine thick enough to float an egg in.

All this was a part of the preparations for the long Dales winters. Nowadays the deep-freeze has changed all that—and even if you haven't a deep-freeze, you can buy fresh meat and vegetables all the year round. Of course, some folk say the old ways of making good country food have gone now these new gadgets are with us, but that's not true; my dad, Sam Pearson, said the Aga wouldn't last a week the day we first brought it to the farm! I may not cook oatcakes on a bakestone by the fire, like my mother did, but I still do my baking and preserving the way she taught me; and to me a leg of lamb or a joint of mutton's the same whether you cook it in May or December.

Many of the recipes in this book I got from my mother, who got them from her mother before that; but since I was asked to compile a special Emmerdale cookbook, I've asked other members of the family and friends to give me some favourite recipes of theirs. Dolly provided some quite fancy ones, like Coq au Vin and Boeuf Bourguignonne, which is also a favourite of Pat's, who, in turn, was delighted to add her own specialities too. My dad, Sam, insisted I include Kidney Soup and Lancashire Hot-Pot, which I've cooked for him more times than I can remember. Young Jackie was adamant about including my Toad in the Hole, Bubble and Squeak and Queen of Puddings; while Jack's favourite dish, Steak and Kidney Pie, was also at the top of Joe's list. And now that Sandie enjoys baking so much, she too gave me some of her own favourites. I even raided Amos Brearly's recipe book for a few of his specialities—Trout and Almonds and Boiled Beef and Dumplings, while Henry Wilks didn't mind admitting he also enjoyed cooking certain dishes. And finally, believe it or not, Seth Armstrong agreed to give me recipes based on his extensive knowledge of the local game!

I've really enjoyed gathering these recipes together and I hope you'll enjoy them as much as we all do—and I hope too that you'll find that the traditions and special qualities of good farmhouse cooking from the Yorkshire Dales are all reflected in this book.

Warming Farmhouse Soups

MY OXTAIL SOUP

I make it specially for Jackie

Serves 4 – 6

25 g/1 oz beef dripping
1 oxtail, jointed
1 medium-sized onion, sliced
1 large carrot, sliced
1 turnip, sliced
1 stick of celery, sliced
1.2 litres/2 pints water *or* basic stock
1 x 5 ml spoon/1 teaspoon salt
bouquet garni
6 black peppercorns
25 g/1 oz plain flour

Heat the dripping in a saucepan. Add half the jointed tail and fry until the meat is browned. Lift out the meat and reserve the fat in the pan. Fry the vegetables in the hot dripping until golden-brown, then remove.

Put all the oxtail and the fried vegetables into a large saucepan. Add the water or stock, and heat very slowly to boiling point. Add the salt, bouquet garni and peppercorns. Cover and simmer very gently for 3 – 4 hours.

Meanwhile, stir the flour into the dripping in the saucepan and fry gently until golden-brown. Strain the soup. Remove all the meat from the bones. Return some of the smaller pieces of meat and any small slices of carrot to the soup. Whisk in the browned flour. Re-heat the soup to boiling point, whisking all the time. Re-season if required.

Jackie always enjoys a bowl of soup, particularly in Winter

BASIC STOCK

Makes 1.2 litres/2 pints (approx)

900 g/2 lb cooked or raw bones of any meat or poultry, chopped into manageable pieces *or* cooked or raw meat trimmings, giblets and bacon rinds
salt
450 g/1 lb onions, carrots, celery and leeks, sliced
1 bay leaf
4 black peppercorns

Put the bones into a saucepan, cover with cold water and add 1 x 2.5 ml spoon/½ teaspoon salt for each 1.2 litres/2 pints of water used. Heat slowly to simmering point. Add the other ingredients, and simmer, uncovered, for at least 3 hours.
Strain the stock and cool quickly by standing the pan in chilled water. When cold, skim off the fat. If the stock is not required at once, keep it cold. Use within 24 hours, or within 3 days if kept in a refrigerator. Reboil before use.

MULLIGATAWNY SOUP

Serves 4

25 g/1 oz butter *or* margarine

1 medium-sized onion, finely chopped

1 small cooking apple, finely chopped

2 x 15 ml spoons/2 tablespoons curry powder

25 g/1 oz plain flour

1.2 litres/2 pints water

450 g/1 lb lean mutton *or* shin of beef, cut into small pieces

1 large carrot, sliced

1/2 small parsnip, sliced

bouquet garni

1 x 2.5 ml spoon/1/2 teaspoon lemon juice

1 x 2.5 ml spoon/1/2 teaspoon salt

1/2 x 2.5 ml spoon/1/4 teaspoon black treacle *or* extra lemon juice

Melt the fat in a large saucepan and fry the onion and apple quickly for 2 – 3 minutes. Add the curry powder, cook gently for 2 minutes, then stir in the flour. Gradually add the water and stir until boiling. Add the meat. Add the carrot and parsnip to the pan with the bouquet garni, lemon juice and salt, and simmer until the meat is very tender – This will take 3 hours for mutton and 4 hours for shin of beef.
Taste the soup, and add the black treacle or more lemon juice to obtain a flavour that is neither predominantly sweet nor acid. Strain the soup. Dice some of the meat finely, add to the soup and re-heat.
Serve with boiled long-grain rice.

BECKINDALE BROTH

Serves 4 – 6

25 g/1 oz butter *or* margarine

1 medium-sized carrot, thinly sliced

1 small turnip, thinly sliced

1 medium-sized onion, thinly sliced

1 clove of garlic, crushed

1.2 litres/2 pints basic stock (see page 13)

1 x 2.5 ml spoon/1/2 teaspoon salt

1/2 small cabbage, shredded

salt and pepper

grated nutmeg

a sprig of parsley, chopped

a few chives, chopped

6 thin slices French bread

Melt the fat in a large saucepan, add the carrot, turnip, onion and garlic, cover and fry gently for 10 minutes. Heat the stock to boiling point and add to the vegetables in the pan with the salt. Cover and simmer for 30 minutes.
Add the cabbage to the broth, cover and simmer for a further 20 minutes. Season to taste with salt, pepper and a little nutmeg. Add the parsley and chives. Keep over very low heat while toasting the bread slices until golden. Put one slice in each soup bowl and pour the broth over them.
Serve with grated cheese.

KIDNEY SOUP

Dad would have this every day if he could!

Serves 4

225 g/8 oz ox kidney, cut into small pieces

25 g/1 oz plain flour

25 g/1 oz dripping *or* lard

1 medium-sized onion, sliced

1 large carrot, sliced

1 small turnip, sliced

1 stick of celery, sliced

1.2 litres/2 pints basic stock (see page 13)

bouquet garni

6 black peppercorns

salt

a little extra stock *or* cold water

Coat the kidney with flour. Keep any remaining flour to thicken the soup at the end. Heat the fat in a large saucepan. Fry the kidney lightly until just browned, then remove from the pan. Fry the vegetables in the fat for about 5 minutes until they begin to brown. Drain off any excess fat. Add the stock, bouquet garni and seasoning. Heat to boiling point, cover, reduce the heat, and simmer gently for 2 hours.
Remove the bouquet garni and strain the soup. Reserve a few pieces of kidney for the garnish. Purée the rest of the kidney and add to the soup. Blend any remaining flour with a little stock or water, add it to the soup, and stir until boiling. Reduce the heat and simmer for 5 minutes. Chop the reserved kidney pieces and add to the soup. Re-season if required.

COW-HEEL SOUP

Another of Dad's favourites

Serves 4 – 6

1 prepared cow-heel

1 medium-sized onion, diced

1 large carrot, diced

1 stick of celery, diced

bouquet garni

salt and pepper

25 g/1 oz fine tapioca

1 x 5 ml spoon/1 teaspoon lemon juice

a pinch of grated nutmeg

1 x 15 ml spoon/1 tablespoon chopped parsley

Put the cow-heel in a saucepan, cover with cold water, and heat slowly to boiling point to blanch. Pour off and reserve the water, then divide the cow-heel into pieces. Put in a large saucepan with the water and heat to boiling point. Add the vegetables to the pan with the bouquet garni. Cover and simmer for 3½ hours.
Remove the cow-heel and strain the soup. Remove some meat from the bone and dice it. Season the soup to taste. Re-heat to boiling point and sprinkle in the tapioca. Cook until the grain is quite clear and soft. Add the pieces of meat, the lemon juice, nutmeg and parsley.

Dad also enjoys soups greatly

Emmerdale Hotch Potch

EMMERDALE HOTCH POTCH

Serves 8

900 g/2 lb scrag and middle neck of lamb *or* mutton
1.5 litres/2½ pints water
1 x 10 ml spoon/1 dessertspoon salt
bouquet garni
1 medium-sized carrot, diced
1 small turnip, diced
6 spring onions, cut into thin rings
1 small lettuce, shredded
100 g/4 oz shelled young broad beans *or* runner beans, sh.edded
100 g/4 oz cauliflower florets
175 g/6 oz shelled peas
salt and pepper
1 x 15 ml spoon/1 tablespoon chopped parsley

Remove the meat from the bone and cut the meat into small pieces. Put the bone and meat into a large saucepan, add the water, and heat very slowly to simmering point. Add the salt and the bouquet garni, cover and simmer very gently for 30 minutes.

Add the carrot, turnip and spring onions to the pan, cover and simmer for 1½ hours. Add the rest of the vegetables, cover and simmer for a further 30 minutes, then season to taste. Skim off the fat and remove the bouquet garni and the bones. Add the chopped parsley just before serving.

CALF'S FOOT BROTH

A recipe first made by my grandmother

Serves 4 – 6

1 calf's foot
1.8 litres/3 pints water
2 – 3 strips lemon rind
salt and pepper
egg yolks
milk

Put the calf's foot into a large saucepan with the water, heat to simmering point, cover and simmer gently for 3 hours.

Strain the broth through a colander or a sieve into a basin and leave to cool. When cold, skim the fat. Re-heat the broth with the lemon rind until sufficiently flavoured, then remove the lemon rind and season to taste. For each 300 ml/½ pint broth, allow 1 egg yolk and 4 x 5 ml spoons/ 4 tablespoons milk. Beat together the egg yolks and milk until well blended, then beat into a little hot soup, and fold into the rest of the soup. Stir over low heat until thickened. Do not allow the broth to boil or it will curdle. Serve hot.

CHICKEN BROTH

Jack never seems to get enough of this!

Serves 8

1 small boiling fowl, jointed *or* 1 chicken carcass, broken up with some flesh left on it
giblets of the bird
1 x 5 ml spoon/1 teaspoon salt
1 medium-sized onion, halved
2 medium-sized carrots, diced
1 stick of celery, diced
½ x 2.5 ml spoon/¼ teaspoon ground pepper
a blade of mace
bouquet garni
a strip of lemon rind
25 g/1 oz long-grain rice
1 x 15 ml spoon/1 tablespoon chopped parsley

Put the boiling fowl or carcass into a large saucepan with the giblets and cover with cold water. Add the salt, and heat slowly to simmering point. Add the vegetables to the pan with the pepper, mace, bouquet garni and lemon rind. Cover and simmer gently for 3 – 3½ hours if using a raw boiling fowl, or for 1½ hours if using a chicken carcass.

Strain the broth through a colander, then skim off the fat. Return the broth to the pan and re-heat to simmering point. Sprinkle the rice into the broth, then cover and simmer for a further 15 – 20 minutes until the rice is cooked.

Some of the meat can be chopped finely and added to the broth, the rest can be used in made-up dishes, eg a fricassée. Just before serving the broth, re-season if required, and add the chopped parsley.

COCK-A-LEEKIE

Serves 8

100 g/4 oz prunes
1 small boiling fowl with giblets
900 g/2 lb beef marrow bones, chopped into manageable pieces
3 rashers streaky bacon, without rinds, chopped
2 x 5 ml spoons/2 teaspoons salt
450 g/1 lb leeks, cut into thin rings
½ x 2.5 ml spoon/¼ teaspoon pepper
bouquet garni

Soak the prunes overnight in cold water, then stone them. Put the fowl, giblets, marrow bones and bacon into a deep pan, cover with cold water, add the salt, and heat very slowly to simmering point. Reserve 4 x 15 ml spoons/4 tablespoons of the leeks and add the remaining leeks, the pepper and bouquet garni to the pan. Cover and simmer gently for about 3 hours or until the fowl is tender.

Remove the fowl, carve off the meat and cut it into fairly large serving pieces. Strain the liquid, then return the pieces to the soup with the prunes and the remaining leeks. Simmer very gently for 30 minutes until the prunes are just tender but not broken. Re-season if required. Serve the soup with the prunes.

CREAM OF CHICKEN SOUP

Always asked for by Joe

Serves 4 – 6

25 g/1 oz cornflour
150 ml/¼ pint milk
1.2 litres/2 pints chicken stock
50 g/2 oz cooked chicken, diced
salt and pepper
1 x 5 ml spoon/1 teaspoon lemon juice
a pinch of grated nutmeg
2 egg yolks
2 x 15 ml spoons/2 tablespoons single cream

Blend the cornflour with a little of the milk. Heat the stock to boiling point and stir into the blended cornflour. Return the mixture to the pan and re-heat to boiling point, stirring all the time. Reduce the heat, cover and simmer for 20 minutes. Add the chicken, and heat in the soup. Season to taste, and add the lemon juice and nutmeg. Beat the yolks with the rest of the milk and the cream, then beat in a little hot soup, and fold into the rest of the soup. Heat until it thickens, but do not allow it to boil.

GAME SOUP

Seth provides the game and I provide the other ingredients

Serves 4

remains of 1 roast pheasant
25 g/1 oz butter *or* margarine
50 g/2 oz lean bacon, without rinds and cubed
1.2 litres/2 pints basic stock (see page 13)
1 medium-sized onion, sliced
1 large carrot, sliced
bouquet garni
a blade of mace
1 chicken liver
25 g/1 oz flour
4 x 10 ml spoons/4 dessertspoons port *or* sherry
salt and pepper

GARNISH

bread croûtons

Cut any large pieces of meat from the carcass of the pheasant. Melt the fat in a frying pan and fry the game pieces and bacon lightly. Put to one side. Put the stock and game bones in a large stewpan and add the vegetables, bouquet garni and mace. Heat to boiling point, cover and simmer for 2 – 2½ hours. Add the liver to the pan and simmer for another 15 minutes. Lift out the liver, then strain the soup through a colander into a clean pan. Discard the bones.

Purée the liver and reserved meat and bacon with a little of the fat in the pan if a rich purée is wanted. Re-heat the rest of the fat in the pan, stir in the flour, and cook for 4 – 5 minutes, stirring all the time, until nut brown. Stir the roux gradually into the meat purée. Heat the soup to boiling point, then draw the pan off the heat. Stir in the purée mixture in small spoonfuls. Return to gentle heat and stir until the soup thickens to the preferred consistency. Add the port or sherry, and season to taste. Garnish with bread croûtons.

Thick soups and pies are great favourites of Joe

BARLEY SOUP

Enjoyed by all of us, come Autumn

Serves 4 – 6

40 g/1½ oz barley

300 ml/½ pint milk

1.2 litres/2 pints basic stock (see page 13)

25 g/1 oz butter

1 x 2.5 ml spoon/½ teaspoon yeast extract

salt and pepper

grated nutmeg

GARNISH

bread croûtons

Blend the barley with the milk in a saucepan. Heat
the stock with the butter and the yeast extract to
boiling point, then stir it into the barley and milk.
Return the mixture to the pan and simmer until the
barley thickens and becomes clear, stirring all the
time. Season to taste, and add a pinch of nutmeg.
Garnish with bread croûtons.

BROWN ONION SOUP

Serves 6

25 g/1 oz butter *or* margarine

3 large Spanish onions, chopped

1.2 litres/2 pints brown stock

bouquet garni

salt and pepper

2 x 10 ml spoons/2 dessertspoons flour for each
600 ml/1 pint puréed soup

cold stock, water *or* milk

Melt the fat in a large saucepan, add the onions,
and fry gently for about 20 minutes until browned.
Add the stock, bouquet garni and seasoning to
taste. Heat to boiling point, reduce the heat, and
simmer gently until the onions are quite soft. Do
not overcook. Remove the bouquet garni.
Purée the vegetables and liquid. Weigh the flour
in the correct proportion and blend it with a little
cold stock, water or milk, then stir it into the soup.
Bring to the boil, stirring all the time, and cook for
5 minutes. Re-season if required.

BROWN STOCK

Makes 1.8 litres/3 pints (approx)

450 g/1 lb beef *or* veal marrow bones, chopped into
manageable pieces

450 g/1 lb shin of beef, cut into small pieces

1.8 litres/3 pints cold water

1 x 5ml spoon/1 teaspoon salt

1 medium-sized onion, sliced

1 medium-sized carrot, sliced

1 stick of celery, sliced

bouquet garni

1 x 2.5 ml spoon/½ teaspoon black peppercorns

Brown the bones and meat in a roasting tin in a hot
oven, 220°C/425°F/Gas 7, for 30 – 40 minutes,
turning them occasionally.
Put the browned bones and meat in a large
saucepan with the water and salt. Add the
vegetables with the bouquet garni and
peppercorns. Heat slowly to boiling point, skim
well, and cover the pan with a tight-fitting lid.
Reduce the heat and simmer very gently for
4 hours.
Strain the stock through a fine sieve and leave to
cool. When cold, skim off the fat. Use as required.

MY GREEN PEA SOUP WITH LIVER DUMPLINGS

Serves 4

550 g/1¼ lb green peas in the pod

1 x 10 ml spoon/1 dessertspoon butter

1 medium-sized onion, sliced

600 ml/1 pint white stock (see page 21)

a few spinach leaves, roughly chopped

a sprig of mint

a few parsley stalks

2 x 10 ml spoons/2 dessertspoons cornflour for each 600 ml/1 pint puréed soup

cold stock, water *or* milk

salt and pepper

sugar

a few drops green food colouring (optional)

4 x 15 ml spoons/4 tablespoons single cream

Shell the peas and wash half the pods. Melt the fat in a large saucepan, add the washed pods and the sliced onion, and fry very gently for 10 minutes. Add the stock and heat to boiling point. Add the peas, spinach leaves and herbs. Simmer for 10 – 20 minutes or until the peas are just cooked. Purée the vegetables and liquid, then measure the soup, and return it to a clean pan. Weigh the cornflour in the correct proportion and blend it with a little cold stock, water or milk. Stir it into the soup. Bring to the boil, stirring all the time, and cook for 5 minutes. Season to taste with salt, pepper and sugar, then add the colouring, if liked. Stir in the cream at boiling point, off the heat. Serve with Liver Dumplings.

LIVER DUMPLINGS

Makes 30 – 36

2 slices white bread, crusts removed

a little milk *or* water

450 g/1 lb chicken liver, chopped

1 small onion, finely chopped

grated rind of ½ lemon

1 x 5 ml spoon/1 teaspoon chopped parsley

salt and pepper

a pinch of grated nutmeg

2 x 15 ml spoons/2 tablespoons plain flour

2 eggs, beaten

1.8 litres/3 pints water

Soak the bread in the milk or water. Squeeze as dry as possible and add to the liver. Add the onion with the lemon rind, parsley, seasoning, nutmeg and flour, and mix well together. Mix in the eggs, then form the mixture into oval shapes with two dessertspoons.
Meanwhile, heat the water to boiling point in a large pan and gently lower the dumplings into the liquid. Simmer for 15 minutes.

My Green Pea Soup with Liver Dumplings

WHITE STOCK

Makes 2.4 litres/4 pints (approx)

900 g/2 lb knuckle of veal, chopped into
manageable pieces

2.4 litres/4 pints cold water

1 x 10 ml spoon/1 dessertspoon salt

1 x 10 ml spoon/1 dessertspoon white vinegar *or*
lemon juice

1 medium-sized onion, sliced

1 stick of celery, sliced

1 x 2.5 ml spoon/½ teaspoon white peppercorns

a small strip of lemon rind

1 bay leaf

Put the bones in a large pan with the cold water,
salt and vinegar or lemon juice. Heat to boiling
point and skim. Add the vegetables and the other
ingredients. Bring back to the boil, cover, reduce
the heat, and simmer gently for 4 hours.

Strain the stock through a fine sieve and cool it
quickly by standing the pan in chilled water. When
cold, skim off the fat. Use within 24 hours, or
within 3 days if kept in a refrigerator. Reboil before
use. Use as required.

DOLLY'S CELERY SOUP

Serves 4

25 g/1 oz butter *or* margarine

450 g/1 lb outer sticks celery, chopped

1 medium-sized onion, chopped

600 ml/1 pint white stock

25 ml/1 fl oz lemon juice

salt and pepper

150 ml/¼ pint milk

2 x 10 ml spoons/2 dessertspoons cornflour for each
600 ml/1 pint puréed soup

cold stock, water *or* milk

Melt the fat in a large saucepan, add the
vegetables, and fry gently for 5 – 10 minutes
without browning them. Add the stock, lemon juice
and seasoning to taste. Heat to boiling point,
reduce the heat, and simmer gently until the
vegetables are quite soft. Do not overcook.

Purée the vegetables and liquid, then add the
milk, measure the soup, and return it to a clean
pan. Weigh the cornflour in the correct proportion
and blend it with a little cold stock, water or milk,
then stir it into the soup. Cook gently for 5 minutes,
stirring all the time. Re-season if required.

Amos and Henry's Tomato Soup

MY SPECIAL LENTIL SOUP

Serves 6

1.2 litres/2 pints water *or* basic stock (see page 13)
175 g/6 oz red *or* brown lentils
1 x 10 ml spoon/1 dessertspoon bacon fat
a few bacon scraps or rinds, chopped *or* a bacon bone
1 medium-sized onion, sliced
2 sticks celery, sliced
½ small turnip, sliced
1 medium-sized potato, sliced
50 g/2 oz carrots, sliced
bouquet garni
a blade of mace
300 ml/½ pint milk
salt and pepper

Heat the water or stock to boiling point, pour it over the lentils, and leave to soak overnight.
Heat the bacon fat in a large saucepan, add the bacon or bone and the vegetables, and fry gently for 10 minutes. Add the soaked lentils and their liquid, the bouquet garni and mace. Heat to boiling point, cover and simmer for 2 hours or until the lentils are quite soft.
Remove the bouquet garni and bone, if used, and rub the vegetables and cooking liquid through a sieve. Return to a clean pan and add the milk.
Re-heat and season to taste.

AMOS AND HENRY'S TOMATO SOUP

Serves 4

50 g/2 oz butter *or* margarine
550 g/1¼ lb tomatoes, chopped
1 small onion, chopped
1 medium-sized carrot, chopped
1 stick of celery, sliced
25 g/1 oz lean bacon, without rinds and chopped
600 ml/1 pint white stock (see page 21)
bouquet garni
salt and pepper
25 g/1 oz flour
300 ml/½ pint milk
4 x 10 ml spoons/4 dessertspoons single cream

Melt half the fat in a large saucepan, add the vegetables and bacon, and fry gently for 5 minutes. Add the stock and bouquet garni, and season to taste. Heat to boiling point, and simmer gently until the vegetables are soft. Remove the bouquet garni. Rub through a fine sieve.
Using the rest of the fat, melt it in the cleaned saucepan, add the flour and stir over gentle heat for 2 – 3 minutes without allowing it to colour. Gradually add the milk, stirring well. Heat to boiling point, and simmer for 2 – 3 minutes, stirring constantly. Stir in the vegetable purée, re-heat to boiling point, and season to taste. Cool slightly. Add a little of the soup to the single cream, and beat well. Whisk the mixture into the rest of the soup, and heat gently, stirring all the time.

CREAM OF MUSHROOM SOUP

My Jack enjoys anything made with mushrooms

Serves 4

300 ml/½ pint white stock (see page 21)

225 g/8 oz mushroom stalks *or* large mushrooms, chopped

1 medium-sized onion, chopped

25 g/1 oz butter *or* margarine

25 g/1 oz flour

600 ml/1 pint milk

salt and pepper

150 ml/¼ pint single cream

1 egg yolk

GARNISH

chopped parsley

Heat the stock to boiling point in a large saucepan and add the vegetables, reserving a few mushroom pieces for garnish. Cover, and cook until the vegetables are tender, then purée them.
Melt the fat in the cleaned saucepan, add the flour, and stir over gentle heat for 2 – 3 minutes without allowing it to colour. Gradually add the milk, stirring well. Heat to boiling point and simmer for 2 – 3 minutes, stirring constantly. Stir in the vegetable purée, re-heat to boiling point, and season to taste. Cool slightly, then add the reserved mushroom pieces. Add a little of the soup to the cream and yolk, and beat well. Whisk the mixture into the rest of the soup and re-heat gently, stirring all the time. Garnish the finished soup with chopped parsley.

Cream of Mushroom Soup

POTATO SOUP

Jack, Joe and Jackie all hanker for this after a hard day in the fields

Serves 6

50 g/2 oz margarine

900 g/2 lb potatoes, chopped

2 medium-sized onions

2 sticks celery, chopped

1.2 litres/2 pints white stock (see page 21)

bouquet garni

salt and pepper

150 ml/¼ pint milk

a pinch of grated nutmeg

Melt the fat in a large saucepan, add the vegetables, and fry gently for 5 – 10 minutes without browning them. Add the stock, bouquet garni and seasoning to taste. Heat to boiling point, reduce the heat, and simmer gently until the vegetables are quite soft. Do not overcook. Remove the bouquet garni.
Purée the vegetables and liquid, then return to a clean pan. Add the milk and a pinch of grated nutmeg, then bring to the boil, stirring all the time, and cook for 5 minutes. Re-season if required.

Fresh From the River, Dairy and Nest
Fish

MY SPECIAL FRIED COD

Serves 4

100 g/4 oz plain flour
salt and pepper
900 g/2 lb skinned cod fillets, cut into serving portions
oil *or* fat for deep frying

BATTER

225 g/8 oz plain flour, sifted
1 x 15 ml spoon/1 tablespoon vegetable oil
salt and pepper
250 ml/8 fl oz light beer
150 ml/¼ pint water
2 egg whites

Prepare the batter first. Mix the flour with the oil, salt, pepper, beer and water. Whisk well for 3 – 5 minutes, then leave to stand for at least 30 minutes. Before coating the fish, whisk the egg whites until stiff and fold into the batter. Season the 100 g/4 oz flour with salt and pepper, and roll each portion of fish in it, shaking off any excess. Dip immediately into the batter, and fry the fish in deep fat until golden-brown. Drain and serve immediately.

HENRY'S MAÎTRE D'HÔTEL COD

Serves 5 – 6

900 g/2 lb cod fillets (cold leftovers can be used)
100 g/4 oz butter
2 x 15 ml spoons/2 tablespoons chopped onion
1 x 15 ml spoon/1 tablespoon chopped parsley
juice of ½ lemon
salt and pepper

Poach the cod if required, and remove the skin when cool. Separate the flesh into large flakes. Melt the butter in a saucepan, add the onion, and fry for 2 – 3 minutes without browning. Add the fish and sprinkle it with the chopped parsley, lemon juice and a good pinch of salt and pepper. Cook over low heat for 5 minutes, stirring gently all the time.
Serve with boiled potatoes.

Amos' Golden Cod

AMOS'S GOLDEN COD

Serves 4

4 cod cutlets

TOPPING
25 g/1 oz soft margarine

50 g/2 oz mild Cheddar cheese, grated

2 x 15 ml spoons/2 tablespoons milk

salt and pepper

GARNISH
grilled tomatoes

watercress sprigs

Place the fish in a greased shallow flameproof dish and grill under moderate heat for 2 – 3 minutes on one side only.

Meanwhile, prepare the topping. Cream together the margarine and cheese, then work in the milk, a few drops at a time, and season to taste. Turn the fish over, spread the topping on the uncooked side, and return to the grill. Reduce the heat slightly and cook for 10 – 12 minutes until the fish is cooked through and the topping is golden-brown. Serve garnished with grilled halved tomatoes and watercress sprigs.

MY FISH CAKES
Matt particularly enjoys these when he comes to visit

Serves 4

450 g/1 lb cold boiled potatoes

25 g/1 oz butter

2 x 15 ml spoons/2 tablespoons cream

275 g/10 oz cooked white fish, skinned, boned and flaked

1 x 15 ml spoon/1 tablespoon finely chopped parsley

salt and pepper

flour for coating

fat for shallow frying

Mash the potatoes until smooth, then mix in the butter and cream. Add the flaked fish and parsley, and season to taste. Divide the mixture into eight portions, and shape into flat, round cakes. Season the flour and dip each cake in it. Shallow fry for 6 – 8 minutes, turning once.

Dolly's Individual Fish Pies

DOLLY'S INDIVIDUAL FISH PIES

Serves 4

50 g/2 oz butter
2 small onions, chopped
50 g/2 oz flour
600 ml/1 pint milk
100 g/4 oz Cheddar cheese, grated
a good pinch of dry mustard
salt and pepper
550 g/1¼ lb cooked white fish, flaked
675 g/1½ lb mashed potato

Melt the butter in a pan and cook the onions until soft. Sprinkle with the flour, and cook for 1 minute. Gradually add the milk and bring to the boil, stirring all the time. Add the cheese, and season to taste with the mustard and salt and pepper. Stir the fish into the sauce, then spoon into four individual dishes.
Put the potato in a piping bag fitted with a star nozzle and, starting from the centre, pipe outwards to cover the pies. Place the dishes under a low grill and heat until golden-brown.
Serve with a side salad.

HERRINGS WITH MUSTARD SAUCE

One of our Friday specialities

Serves 4

4 herrings, heads removed and boned
2 x 5 ml spoons/2 teaspoons lemon juice
salt and pepper
1 x 10 ml spoon/1 dessertspoon dry mustard
2 egg yolks
50 g/2 oz butter, cut into small pieces
2 x 15 ml spoons/2 tablespoons double cream
1 x 15 ml spoon/1 tablespoon chopped capers
1 x 15 ml spoon/1 tablespoon chopped gherkin

Sprinkle the fish with lemon juice and season well. Grill, using moderate heat, for 3 – 5 minutes on each side. Keep hot.
Put the mustard and egg yolks in a basin and whisk over a pan of hot water until creamy. Whisk in the butter in small quantities. When the sauce thickens, remove from the heat and stir in the cream. Add the capers and gherkin, and season well. Serve the sauce hot with the herrings.

MY MOTHER'S FISH PUDDING

Serves 4 – 5

100 g/4 oz shredded suet
450 g/1 lb white fish, filletted and finely chopped
50 g/2 oz soft white breadcrumbs
parsley
salt and pepper
a few drops anchovy essence
150 ml/¼ pint milk
2 eggs, lightly beaten

Mix together the suet, fish, breadcrumbs, parsley, seasoning and anchovy essence. Lightly beat together the milk and eggs and stir into the mixture. Place in a greased 600 ml/1 pint basin, cover with greased paper or foil, and steam gently for 1½ hours.

PAT'S HALIBUT, ORANGE AND WATERCRESS SALAD

Serves 4

4 – 6 halibut steaks

600 ml/1 pint court bouillon

1 lettuce, shredded

mayonnaise

GARNISH
orange slices

watercress sprigs

Poach the fish steaks in the court bouillon for 7 – 10 minutes. Lift out, drain well and leave to cool. Remove the skin. Arrange some of the lettuce on a salad dish. Coat the fish with the mayonnaise, and arrange on the lettuce. Garnish with orange slices, the remaining lettuce and watercress sprigs.

COURT BOUILLON

water

600 ml/1 pint dry white wine *or* dry cider for each 1.2 litres/2 pints water

2 x 15 ml spoons/2 tablespoons white wine vinegar for each 1.2 litres/2 pints water

2 large carrots, sliced

2 large onions, sliced

2 – 3 sticks celery, chopped

parsley stalks, crushed

1 bouquet garni for each 1.2 litres/2 pints water

a few peppercorns

salt and pepper

Put the liquids in a large pan, then add the vegetables with the remaining ingredients. Simmer for 30 minutes, leave to cool, then strain and use as required.

Pat's Halibut, Orange and Watercress Salad

PAT'S SKATE IN BLACK BUTTER

Serves 3 – 4

1 – 2 skate wings, cut into serving portions
1.2 litres/2 pints court bouillon (see page 27)

BLACK BUTTER
25 g/1 oz butter
salt and pepper
2 x 15 ml spoons/2 tablespoons capers
2 x 10 ml spoons/2 dessertspoons chopped parsley
75 ml/3 fl oz wine vinegar

Put the fish in a deep frying pan and cover with the court bouillon. Bring to the boil, reduce the heat, cover and simmer for 15 – 20 minutes. Lift out the fish, drain, and gently scrape away the skin. Place in an ovenproof dish and keep hot.

To make the black butter, pour off the stock, put in the butter and heat until it is a rich golden-brown colour. Spoon it quickly over the fish, season with salt and pepper, and scatter the capers and chopped parsley over the fish. Add the vinegar to the pan, heat quickly, and pour over the fish. Serve immediately.

Pat's Skate in Black Butter

Mackerel with Gooseberry Sauce

MACKEREL WITH GOOSEBERRY SAUCE
Another favourite Friday dish

Serves 4

flour for coating
salt and pepper
8 mackerel fillets
50 g/2 oz butter
juice of 1 lemon
25 g/1 oz parsley, chopped

SAUCE
400 g/14 oz gooseberries
50 ml/2 fl oz dry still cider
25 g/1 oz butter
1 x 15 ml spoon/1 tablespoon caster sugar

Make the sauce first. Poach the gooseberries in the cider and butter until tender. Sieve to make a smooth purée, then add the sugar.

Meanwhile, season the flour with salt and pepper. Dip the fish fillets in the flour. Heat the butter in a frying pan and fry the fillets gently for 5 – 7 minutes, turning once. Remove them, arrange on a serving plate and keep hot. Reserve the butter in the pan.

Heat the gooseberry sauce in a saucepan and keep hot. Add the remaining butter to the pan, and heat until light brown. Add the lemon juice and chopped parsley, and pour this over the fish. Serve the gooseberry sauce separately.

ABOVE Dolly's Sweet and Sour Prawns

BELOW RIGHT Stuffed Plaice

DOLLY'S SWEET AND SOUR PRAWNS

Serves 4

225 g/8 oz peeled prawns

1 x 15 ml spoon/1 tablespoon medium-dry sherry

salt and pepper

2 x 15 ml spoons/2 tablespoons oil

2 onions, cut into rings

2 green peppers, cut into rings

150 ml/¼ pint chicken stock

225 g/8 oz canned pineapple pieces

1 x 15 ml spoon/1 tablespoon cornflour

2 x 15 ml spoons/2 tablespoons soy sauce

150 ml/¼ pint white wine vinegar

75 g/3 oz sugar

GARNISH

unpeeled prawns

Marinate the prawns in the sherry for 30 minutes and season well. Heat the oil in a saucepan and fry the onions and peppers gently until tender. Add the stock, and drain. Add the pineapple, cover and cook for 3 – 5 minutes. Blend together the cornflour, soy sauce, vinegar and sugar, and add to the mixture. Stir until thickened, then add the prawns, and cook for 1 minute. Serve hot on a bed of boiled rice, and garnish with unpeeled prawns.

STUFFED PLAICE

Dad is very partial to this

Serves 4

4 small plaice

25 g/1 oz butter

STUFFING

100 g/4 oz mild Cheddar cheese, grated

50 g/2 oz soft white breadcrumbs

1 x 5 ml spoon/1 teaspoon dry mustard

salt and pepper

1 x 10 ml spoon/1 dessertspoon mixed dried herbs

juice of ½ lemon

2 x 15 ml spoons/2 tablespoons beaten egg

GARNISH

lemon wedges

parsley sprigs

Make a cut down the centre of the entire length of the fish as for filletting. Loosen the flesh from the bone on each side of the cut, but do not detach it.
Make the stuffing. Mix the cheese with the crumbs, mustard, seasoning, herbs, lemon juice and beaten egg.
Raise the two loose flaps of the fish and fill the pockets with the stuffing. Place the stuffed fish in a buttered oven-to-table baking dish, dot with the butter, and cover loosely with foil. Cook in a fairly hot oven, 190°C/375°F/Gas 5, for 20 – 30 minutes. Garnish with lemon wedges and parsley sprigs.

FRIED PLAICE WITH HERBS

Amos and Henry often eat this for their Friday lunch

Serves 4

450 g/1 lb plaice fillets
salt and pepper
50 g/2 oz lettuce *or* other salad greens, chopped
juice of $\frac{1}{2}$ lemon
1 x 15 ml spoon/1 tablespoon vegetable oil
oil *or* fat for shallow frying

BATTER

100 g/4 oz plain flour, sifted
2 x 15 ml spoons/2 tablespoons vegetable oil
a pinch of salt
150 ml/$\frac{1}{4}$ pint warm water (approx)
2 egg whites

GARNISH

parsley sprigs

Prepare the batter first. Mix the flour with the oil, salt and water. Whisk well to remove any lumps, then leave to stand for 30 minutes. Before coating the fish, whisk the egg whites until stiff and fold into the batter.

Cut the fish fillets into slices 1.25 cm/$\frac{1}{2}$ inch thick and 5 – 7.5 cm/2 – 3 inches long. Sprinkle with salt, pepper and the chopped greens. Pour the lemon juice over the fish, add the oil and leave to stand for 15 – 20 minutes.

Dip each piece of fish in the batter. Heat the fat in a frying pan and fry the fish for 10 – 15 minutes until crisp and golden-brown, then drain. Serve in a pyramid on a heated dish, and garnish with sprigs of parsley.

Serve with a mayonnaise sauce with chopped gherkins.

AMOS'S TROUT WITH ALMONDS

Serves 4

100g /4 oz butter
4 trout
salt and pepper
juice of $\frac{1}{2}$ lemon
50 g/2 oz flaked blanched almonds
150 ml/$\frac{1}{4}$ pint double cream
3 egg yolks

GARNISH

parsley sprigs

Melt the butter in a grill pan under medium heat. Lay the trout in the pan, season, and sprinkle with lemon juice. Grill for 5 minutes, then turn the fish. Sprinkle with most of the almonds, spread the rest at the side of the pan, and continue grilling for a further 3 – 5 minutes until the trout are tender and the almonds are browned. Drain, then put the almonds to one side.

Mix the cream with the yolks and put into a small pan with any juices from the grill pan. Heat gently, stirring well, until thickened; do not let the mixture boil.

Lay the trout on a serving dish, and spoon the cream sauce over them. Garnish with the reserved almonds and with sprigs of parsley.

Amos and Henry take turns to cook their meals

JUGGED KIPPERS

Serves 4

4 kippers

GARNISH

4 pats chilled Maître d'Hôtel butter

Put the kippers, tail end up, in a tall, heatproof jug. Pour boiling water over the whole fish except the tails. Cover the jug with a cloth, and leave to stand for 5 minutes. Tilt the jug gently over a sink, and drain off the water. Do not try to pull the kippers out by their tails. Serve them on warmed plates, topped with pats of Maître d'Hôtel butter.

MAÎTRE D'HÔTEL BUTTER

Makes 50 g/2 oz

2 – 4 large sprigs parsley, blanched and finely chopped

50 g/2 oz softened butter

salt

a small pinch of pepper

a few drops lemon juice

Work the parsley into the butter with the seasonings and lemon juice. Use at once, or pot and chill until required.

Cheese and Eggs

HENRY'S YORKSHIRE RAREBIT

Serves 4

25 g/1 oz butter *or* margarine

1 x 15 ml spoon/1 tablespoon flour

3 x 15 ml spoons/3 tablespoons milk and 2 x 15 ml spoons/2 tablespoons ale *or* beer

1 x 5 ml spoon/1 teaspoon French mustard

a few drops Worcestershire sauce

100 – 175 g/4 – 6 oz Cheddar cheese, grated

salt and pepper

4 slices bread, crusts removed

butter for spreading

4 rashers cooked bacon, rinds removed

Melt the fat in a pan, and stir in the flour. Cook together for 2 – 3 minutes, stirring all the time; do not let the flour colour. Stir in the milk and blend to a smooth, thick mixture, then stir in the ale or beer, the mustard and Worcestershire sauce. Add the cheese little by little, stir in, and season to taste. Remove from the heat as soon as well blended. Toast the bread lightly on both sides. Butter one side well and spread the cheese mixture on the buttered sides. Grill briefly, using high heat to brown the surface of the cheese mixture. Add the bacon rashers and grill lightly. Serve immediately.

Henry's recipe for Yorkshire Rarebit is one that was first given to him by his wife

HENRY'S MACARONI CHEESE

Serves 3 – 4

| 125 g/5 oz elbow cut macaroni |
| 600 ml/1 pint white sauce |
| 100 g/4 oz Cheddar cheese, grated |
| salt and pepper |
| 25 g/1 oz butter |

Cook the macaroni in boiling salted water as directed, then drain well. Meanwhile, heat the white sauce, and mix together in a pan with the macaroni and 75 g/3 oz of the cheese. Season to taste. Heat thoroughly for 1 – 2 minutes, then put the mixture in a greased 750 ml/1¼ pint pie dish. Sprinkle with the remaining cheese, and dot with the butter. Cook in a hot oven, 220°C/425°F/Gas 7, for 20 minutes to brown the cheese.

WHITE SAUCE

Makes 600 ml/1 pint

| 50 g/2 oz butter *or* margarine |
| 50 g/2 oz plain flour |
| 600 ml/1 pint milk |
| salt and pepper |

Put the fat, flour and milk into a saucepan, and whisk over moderate heat until the sauce comes to the boil. Reduce the heat and cook for 3 – 4 minutes, whisking all the time, until the sauce has thickened and is smooth and glossy. Season to taste. Use as required.

DOLLY'S CHEESE FLAN

Serves 4 – 6

| 75 g/3 oz Cheddar cheese, grated |
| 2 eggs |
| 250 ml/8 fl oz milk |
| a pinch of salt |
| Cayenne pepper |

CHEESE PASTRY

| 175 g/6 oz plain flour |
| a pinch of dry mustard |
| a pinch of salt |
| a pinch of Cayenne pepper |
| 75 g/3 oz butter |
| 75 g/3 oz Cheddar cheese, finely grated |
| 1 egg yolk |
| 1 x 15 ml spoon/1 tablespoon cold water |

Prepare the cheese pastry first. Sift together the flour and seasonings into a bowl, then rub in the butter until the mixture resembles fine breadcrumbs. Add the cheese, yolk and enough cold water to form a stiff dough.
Roll out the pastry on a lightly floured surface and use it to line a 20 cm/8 inch flan ring about 2.5 cm/1 inch deep. Bake blind until set, then cool. Whisk together the cheese, eggs, milk and seasonings. Pour into the flan shell, and bake in a fairly hot oven, 190°C/375°F/Gas 5, for 25 – 35 minutes or until firm in the centre and golden-brown.

Scotch Eggs

SCOTCH EGGS

*I often give these to Joe for his lunch when he's working.
All that outdoor air makes him very hungry*

Makes 4

225 g/8 oz sausage-meat
1 egg
2 x 5 ml spoons/2 teaspoons water
1 x 15 ml spoon/1 tablespoon flour
salt and pepper
4 hard-boiled eggs
50 g/2 oz soft white breadcrumbs
oil for deep frying

Divide the sausage-meat into four equal pieces. On a lightly floured surface, roll each piece into a circle 12.5 cm/5 inches in diameter. Beat the egg with the water. Season the flour with salt and pepper and toss the hard-boiled eggs in it. Place an egg in the centre of each circle of sausage-meat and mould evenly round the egg, making sure it fits closely. Seal the joins with the beaten egg, and pinch well together. Mould each Scotch egg into a good shape, brush it all over with beaten egg, and then toss it in the breadcrumbs, covering the surface evenly. Press in the crumbs firmly. Fry the eggs in deep fat until golden-brown, then drain on soft kitchen paper. Cut in half lengthways and serve hot or cold.

As the sausage-meat is raw, it is important that the frying should not be hurried.

DOLLY'S EGGS FLORENTINE

Serves 4

900 g/2 lb fresh spinach
1 x 15 ml spoon/1 tablespoon butter
salt and pepper
4 eggs
100 g/4 oz Cheddar cheese, finely grated

Put the spinach into a saucepan with just the water that clings to the washed leaves, then cover and heat gently. Cook for 10 – 15 minutes, turning the spinach occasionally. When it is tender, drain thoroughly, and chop. Re-heat with the butter and a little salt and pepper. Put into a greased ovenproof dish, and make four hollows in the surface. Break an egg into each hollow, season, and sprinkle the cheese over the eggs. Cook in a fairly hot oven, 190°C/375°F/Gas 5, for 12 – 15 minutes until the eggs are lightly set.

Beckindale's Favourite Main Courses

Meat

PAT'S BEEF CROQUETTES

Serves 4

25 g/1 oz cooking fat
25 g/1 oz onions, finely chopped
25 g/1 oz flour
150 ml/¼ pint brown stock (see page 19)
225 g/8 oz cooked beef, minced
salt and pepper
1 x 5 ml spoon/1 teaspoon chopped parsley
1 x 5 ml spoon/1 teaspoon any bottled savoury sauce
50g/2 oz dry white breadcrumbs
2 eggs, beaten
oil *or* fat for deep frying

Melt the fat in a large frying pan and fry the onions for 2 – 3 minutes. Stir in the flour and cook for 1 – 2 minutes. Stir in the stock and heat to boiling point, stirring all the time. Cook for 2 minutes until the sauce thickens, then add the meat, seasoning, parsley and sauce. Stir over the heat for a moment. Turn the mixture on to a plate, level the surface, cover with a second plate, and leave to cool completely.
When cold, divide into eight equal-sized portions. On a floured surface, form into neat cork or roll-shaped pieces. Scatter the breadcrumbs on a sheet of greaseproof paper. Dip each croquette into the beaten egg, brushing it all over to make sure it is evenly covered, then roll it in the crumbs until it is completely covered. Press the crumbs on lightly. Coat each croquette a second time, then fry in deep fat, a few at a time, until crisp and browned all over. Drain well. Keep the first batches hot while cooking the rest.

SHEPHERD'S PIE

Dolly tells me that she can never make enough of this for Matt

Serves 4 – 6

25 g/1 oz dripping
2 medium-sized onions, sliced
1 x 15 ml spoon/1 tablespoon flour
150 ml/¼ pint strong brown stock (see page 19)
550 g/1¼ lb beef mince
salt and freshly ground black pepper
675 g/1½ lb potatoes
a pinch of grated nutmeg
milk
1 – 2 x 15 ml spoons/1 – 2 tablespoons softened butter

Heat the dripping in a saucepan, and fry the onions until softened but not coloured. Stir in the flour, and cook gently for 1 – 2 minutes, stirring all the time. Gradually add the stock, without letting lumps form, and stir until boiling. Reduce the heat, and simmer for 2 – 3 minutes until the sauce thickens. Stir in the mince, cover the pan, and simmer for 20 minutes. Season well, replace the lid, and simmer for 10 minutes longer or until the mince is cooked through and tender.
Meanwhile, boil the potatoes in salted water until tender. Mash them until smooth with a seasoning of salt, pepper, nutmeg, enough milk to make them creamy, and butter. Put the meat and sauce into a greased pie dish, cover with the potato, and score a pattern on the surface with a fork. Cook for 10 – 15 minutes in a hot oven, 220°C/425°F/ Gas 7, until browned on top. Serve hot.

AMOS'S BOILED BEEF WITH VEGETABLES AND DUMPLINGS

Serves 8 – 10

900 g – 1.1 kg/2 – 2½ lb brisket of beef
1 x 5 ml spoon/1 teaspoon salt
3 cloves
10 peppercorns
bouquet garni
3 medium-sized onions, cut into small pieces
4 large carrots, cut into small pieces
2 small turnips, cut into small pieces

SUET DUMPLINGS

225 g/8 oz self-raising flour
100 g/4 oz suet
½ x 2.5 ml spoon/¼ teaspoon salt

Weigh the meat and calculate the cooking time, allowing 25 minutes for each 450 g/1 lb plus 20 minutes extra. Put the meat into a large stewpan, cover with boiling water, and add the salt. Bring the water to the boil again and boil for 5 minutes to seal the surface of the meat. Reduce the heat to simmering point, and skim. Add the cloves, peppercorns and bouquet garni. Cover the pan and simmer for the rest of the calculated cooking time.
About 45 minutes before the end of the cooking time, add the vegetables to the meat and re-heat to simmering point.
Prepare the dumplings. Mix the flour, suet and salt in a bowl, then add enough cold water to make a fairly stiff dough. Divide this mixture into walnut-sized pieces and roll them into balls. Drop them into the pan with the beef, so that they simmer for the final 20 – 30 minutes of the cooking time. Keep the pan covered and turn the dumplings over once during this time.
To serve, remove the bouquet garni. Take out the dumplings and vegetables with a perforated spoon, and arrange them as a border on a large warmed serving dish. Remove any strings from the meat, skewer if necessary, and set it in the centre of the dish. Serve some of the liquid separately in a sauceboat.

Dolly's Beef Salad

DOLLY'S BEEF SALAD

Serves 4

1 Cos *or* Webbs lettuce
1 green pepper, thinly sliced
200 g/7 oz sweetcorn kernels, drained
4 – 5 thin slices roast beef, cut into thin strips
100 g/4 oz button mushrooms, each cut into four

DRESSING

2 x 15 ml spoons/2 tablespoons sunflower oil
1 x 15 ml spoon/1 tablespoon white wine vinegar
1 x 15 ml spoon/1 tablespoon horseradish sauce
salt and pepper

GARNISH

bread croûtons

Tear the lettuce leaves into pieces, and put into a bowl. Add the green pepper, sweetcorn, roast beef and mushrooms.
Whisk together the dressing ingredients, pour on to the salad and mix well. Garnish with bread croûtons.

MY BROWN STEW

One of Joe's favourite hot-pots

Serves 6

25 g/1 oz dripping
675 g/1½ lb stewing steak, cut into pieces 2.5 cm/1 inch thick
1 large onion, sliced
3 x 15 ml spoons/3 tablespoons plain flour
900 ml/1½ pints basic stock (see page 13) *or* water
salt and pepper
bouquet garni
2 large carrots, sliced
1 large turnip, diced

Heat the dripping in a stewpan. Put in the meat, and fry quickly until browned on all sides. Take the meat out of the pan, and put in the onion. Reduce the heat, and fry the onion gently until lightly browned. Stir in the flour and cook slowly until it turns a rich brown colour. Gradually add the stock or water, and heat to boiling point, stirring all the time. Add the seasoning and bouquet garni. Return the meat to the pan, cover with a tight-fitting lid, and simmer for 1½ hours.

Skim off any fat on the surface. Add the carrots and turnip, replace the lid and simmer for another hour or until the meat and vegetables are tender. Again skim off any fat. Re-season if required, and remove the bouquet garni before serving.

HORSERADISH CREAM

Makes 175 ml/6 fl oz (approx)

150 ml/¼ pint double cream
2 x 15 ml spoons/2 tablespoons fresh grated horseradish
1 x 15 ml spoon/1 tablespoon white wine vinegar *or* lemon juice
1 x 10 ml spoon/1 dessertspoon caster sugar
½ x 2.5 ml spoon/¼ teaspoon prepared English mustard
salt and pepper

Whip the cream lightly until semi-stiff. Carefully fold in the other ingredients, then chill until ready to use.

YORKSHIRE PUDDINGS

100 g/4 oz plain flour
½ x 2.5 ml spoon/¼ teaspoon salt
1 egg
300 ml/½ pint milk
lard

Sift the flour and salt into a bowl, make a well in the centre and add the egg. Stir in half the milk, gradually working the flour down from the sides. Beat vigorously until the mixture is smooth and bubbly. Stir in the rest of the milk.
Put small knobs of lard in individual deep patty tins. Place in a preheated hot oven, 220°C/425°F/Gas 7, until the fat is smoking hot.
Half fill the tins with the batter and bake for at least 20 – 25 minutes, depending on the depth of the tins. The puddings will rise high above the tins, and will be almost hollow shells. Do not underbake or they will collapse when taken out of the oven.

THE SUGDEN SUNDAY ROAST

a joint of beef suitable for roasting
salt and pepper
beef dripping (25 g/1 oz per 450 g/1 lb meat approx)

Weigh the meat to calculate the cooking time, allowing 15 minutes for each 450 g/1 lb plus 15 minutes extra. Place the joint, fat side up, on a wire rack if available, in a shallow roasting tin. Season the meat, and rub or spread it with the dripping. Place the roasting tin in the oven and cook in a very hot oven, 230°C/450°F/Gas 8, reducing to fairly hot, 190°C/375°F/Gas 5, after 10 minutes. Transfer the cooked meat to a warmed serving dish, remove any string and secure with a metal skewer if necessary. Keep hot. Drain off the fat from the roasting tin and make a gravy from the sediment, if liked.
Serve with Yorkshire Puddings and Horseradish Cream.

The Family's Sunday Roast

FLAKY PASTRY

Makes 450 g/1 lb (approx)

225 g/8 oz plain flour
$1/2$ x 2.5 ml spoon/$1/4$ teaspoon salt
75 g/3 oz butter
50 g/2 oz lard
1 x 2.5 ml spoon/$1/2$ teaspoon lemon juice
cold water

Sift together the flour and salt into a bowl. Blend together the butter and lard with a round-bladed knife, then divide into four equal portions. Rub one-quarter into the flour, and mix to a soft dough with lemon juice and cold water. On a lightly floured surface, roll the pastry into an oblong strip, keeping the ends square. Divide another quarter of the fat into small knobs, and place them at intervals on the top two-thirds of the pastry. Fold the bottom third up on to the fat and fold the top third down over it. With the rolling-pin, press the edges lightly together to prevent the air escaping. Turn the pastry so that the folded edges are on the left and right. Press the rolling-pin on the pastry at intervals, to make ridges and to distribute the air evenly. Cover the pastry with greaseproof paper and leave to rest in a cool place for 10 minutes. Repeat the rolling and folding three more times; the last rolling will be without fat. Leave the pastry to rest between each rolling. Use as required.

ROUGH PUFF PASTRY

Makes 450 g/1 lb (approx)

225 g/8 oz plain flour
$1/2$ x 2.5 ml spoon/$1/4$ teaspoon salt
75 g/3 oz butter
75 g/3 oz lard
1 x 2.5 ml spoon/$1/2$ teaspoon lemon juice
cold water

Sift together the flour and salt into a bowl. Blend together the fats with a round-bladed knife. Cut the fat into pieces the size of a walnut and add to the flour. Make a well in the centre of the flour, mix in the lemon juice, then gradually add enough cold water to make an elastic dough. On a lightly floured surface, roll into a long strip, keeping the edges square. Fold the bottom third over the centre third, and fold the top third over it. With the rolling-pin, press to seal the edges. Turn the pastry so that the folded edges are on the left and right. Repeat the rolling and folding until the pastry has been folded four times. Allow it to rest in a cool place for 10 minutes between the second and third rollings. Use as required.

Jack's tastes in food reflect both his travels and his origins

STEAK AND KIDNEY PIE

A favourite of Jack and Joe since childhood

Serves 6

3 x 15 ml spoons/3 tablespoons plain flour
1 x 5 ml spoon/1 teaspoon salt
1/2 x 2.5 ml spoon/1/4 teaspoon ground pepper
550 g/1 1/4 lb lean stewing steak, cubed
2 sheep *or* ox kidneys, cut into slices
2 medium-sized onions, chopped
300 ml/1/2 pint (approx) brown stock (see page 19) *or* water
225 g/8 oz prepared flaky *or* rough puff pastry (see page 38)
beaten egg *or* milk for glazing

Mix the flour with the salt and pepper. Toss the cubes of meat and the kidneys in the seasoned flour and put them in a 1.2 litre/2 pint pie dish, piling them higher in the centre Sprinkle the onions between the pieces of meat, then pour in stock or water to quarter-fill the dish.

Roll out the pastry on a lightly floured surface and use to cover the dish. Trim the edge, knock up and flute the edge. Make a small hole in the centre of the lid, and decorate round with leaves of pastry. Make a pastry tassel or rose to cover the hole after baking, if liked. Brush the pastry with the beaten egg or milk.

Bake the pie in a very hot oven, 230°C/450°F/Gas 8, until the pastry is risen and light brown. Bake the tassel or rose blind, if made.

Reduce the oven heat to moderate, 180°C/350°F/Gas 4, and, if necessary, place the pie on a lower shelf. Cover with greaseproof paper to prevent the pastry over-browning, and continue cooking for about 2 hours until the meat is quite tender when tested with a skewer. Just before the pie is cooked, heat the remaining stock. When the pie is cooked, funnel the stock through the hole in the pastry, and cover with the pastry tassel or rose, if made.

Steak and Kidney Pie

Amos and Henry's Specially Seasoned Lamb Chops

AMOS AND HENRY'S SPECIALLY SEASONED LAMB CHOPS

Serves 4 – 8

25 g/1 oz butter
225 g/8 oz button mushrooms
salt and pepper
300 ml/½ pint tomato juice
2 x 5 ml spoons/2 teaspoons paprika
1 x 5 ml spoon/1 teaspoon Worcestershire sauce
4 – 8 lamb cutlets

GARNISH

watercress sprigs

Melt the butter in a large frying pan, add the mushrooms and sprinkle with salt and pepper. Cook for 3 minutes, stirring frequently. Pour in the tomato juice, paprika and Worcestershire sauce, heat to boiling point, then reduce the heat and simmer for 10 minutes.
Meanwhile, put the lamb cutlets in a grill pan, season with salt and pepper, and grill for about 10 minutes or until tender, turning once. Place the meat on a serving dish and cover with the mushrooms and sauce. Garnish with watercress.

HENRY'S LIVER AND BACON

Serves 4 – 6

50 g/2 oz flour
salt and pepper
450 g/1 lb lamb's liver, cut into 1.25 cm/½ inch slices
225 g/8 oz back bacon rashers, without rinds
450 ml/¾ pint brown stock (see page 19)

GARNISH

parsley sprigs

Season the flour with salt and pepper, and dip each slice of liver in the seasoned flour. Cook the bacon rashers in a frying pan, then transfer them to a warmed dish, and keep hot. Fry the slices of liver lightly and quickly in the fat from the bacon until browned on both sides, without hardening or over-cooking them. Transfer the liver to a warmed serving dish, arrange the bacon around it and keep hot.
Drain off all but about 1 x 10 ml spoon/ 1 dessertspoon of fat, stir in the remaining seasoned flour and cook until browned. Gradually add the stock and stir until boiling. Re-season if required. Garnish the liver and bacon with sprigs of parsley and serve the sauce separately.

Henry's Liver and Bacon

Dolly's Sautéed Kidneys

DOLLY'S SAUTÉED KIDNEYS

Serves 4

50 g/2 oz butter
1 small onion, finely chopped
4 sheep's kidneys, thinly sliced
1 x 5 ml spoon/1 teaspoon chopped parsley
150 ml/¼ pint brown sauce
salt and pepper
4 slices fried bread, cut into triangles

GARNISH
chopped parsley

Melt the butter in a frying pan, and fry the onion until just golden-brown. Add the kidney slices and parsley. Stir, and turn over in the fat for 2 – 3 minutes until very lightly fried. Add the brown sauce, and season to taste. Bring the sauce just to the boil. Pour the mixture on to a warmed serving dish. Arrange the fried bread around the edge of the dish, and garnish with chopped parsley. Serve at once.

BROWN SAUCE

Makes 300 ml/½ pint (approx)

25 g/1 oz dripping *or* lard
1 small carrot, sliced
1 medium-sized onion, sliced
25 g/1 oz plain flour
600 ml/1 pint basic stock (see page 13)
salt and pepper

Heat the dripping or lard in a saucepan, then fry the carrot and onion slowly until the onion is golden-brown. Stir in the flour, reduce the heat, and cook the flour very gently until it is also golden-brown. Draw the pan off the heat and gradually add the stock, stirring all the time to prevent lumps forming. Return to moderate heat and stir the sauce until boiling. Reduce the heat, cover and simmer for 30 minutes. Strain the sauce, then season to taste. Use as required.

MY BOILED LEG OF LAMB WITH CAPER SAUCE

Serves 8 – 10

a leg of lamb (1.8 kg/4 lb approx)
1 x 5 ml spoon/1 teaspoon salt
10 black peppercorns
2 medium-sized onions
4 medium-sized carrots
2 turnips
1 – 2 leeks

CAPER SAUCE

450 ml/³⁄₄ pint white sauce (see page 32)
1¹⁄₂ x 15 ml spoons/1¹⁄₂ tablespoons chopped capers
1¹⁄₂ x 5 ml spoons/1¹⁄₂ teaspoons vinegar in which the capers were pickled

Put the meat in a large stewpan with the salt, peppercorns and enough cold water to cover. Heat to boiling point. Skim, reduce the heat, cover the pan with a tight-fitting lid, and simmer over gentle heat for 2¹⁄₂ – 3 hours or until the meat is tender.

Meanwhile, leave the vegetables whole if small, or cut them into large neat pieces. Add them to the meat 45 minutes before the end of the cooking time.

Prepare the Caper Sauce. Heat the white sauce, if necessary, then add the capers and vinegar, and stir well.

Drain the meat and vegetables from the cooking liquid, place on a warmed serving dish, coat with the Caper Sauce, and arrange the vegetables round the meat.

LANCASHIRE HOT POT

Another of Dad's favourites, first cooked for him by my mother

Serves 6

900 g/2 lb potatoes
900 g/2 lb middle neck of lamb *or* mutton, cut into neat cutlets
3 sheep's kidneys, sliced
1 large onion, sliced
salt and pepper
300 ml/¹⁄₂ pint basic stock (see page 13)
25 g/1 oz lard *or* dripping

Slice half the potatoes, and cut the rest into chunks for the top of the casserole. Put a layer in the bottom of a greased, large, deep casserole. Arrange the cutlets on top, slightly overlapping each other, and cover with the kidneys and onion. Season well. Arrange the remainder of the potatoes neatly on top, then pour in the hot stock. Heat the lard or dripping and brush it over the top layer of potatoes. Cover the casserole with a tight-fitting lid and cook in a moderate oven, 180°C/350°F/Gas 4, for about 2 hours or until the meat and potatoes are tender. Remove the lid, increase the oven temperature to hot, 220°C/425°F/Gas 7, and cook for another 20 minutes or until the top layer of potatoes is brown and crisp. Serve from the casserole.

PAT'S LIVER AND POTATO CASSEROLE

Serves 4

50 g/2 oz butter
225 g/8 oz streaky bacon, rinds removed and chopped
350 g/12 oz button onions
flour
salt and pepper
350 g/12 oz lamb's liver, cubed
400 g/14 oz canned tomatoes
1 × 15 ml spoon/1 tablespoon Worcestershire sauce
100 g/4 oz peas
175 g/6 oz sweetcorn kernels
675 g/1½ lb potatoes, sliced and parboiled
25 g/1 oz butter, melted

Melt the butter in a pan, and fry the bacon and onions until the onions begin to soften. Season the flour with salt and pepper, then toss the liver in the flour and add to the bacon mixture. Cook until the liver is lightly browned. Add the tomatoes, Worcestershire sauce, peas and sweetcorn. Season to taste, heat to boiling point and simmer gently until the sauce begins to thicken. Transfer the liver and sauce to a casserole and layer the potato slices over the top. Brush with melted butter. Cook in a moderate oven, 180°C/350°F/Gas 4, for 45 minutes or until the potatoes are golden-brown.

Pat's Liver and Potato Casserole

Sandie's Sausage Rolls

SANDIE'S SAUSAGE ROLLS

Makes 8

225 g/8 oz prepared puff *or* rough puff pastry
(see page 38)

8 sausages *or* 225 g/8 oz sausage-meat

1 egg yolk

Roll out the pastry on a lightly floured surface and cut it into eight equal-sized squares. Skin the sausages if required, or divide the meat into eight equal portions. Form each portion into a roll the same length as a square of pastry. Place one roll of sausage-meat on each pastry square, dampen the edges of the pastry, and fold the pastry over so that they meet. Seal the joined edges and turn the rolls over so that the joints are underneath. Leave the ends of the rolls open. Make three diagonal slits in the top of each roll. Brush the rolls with egg yolk. Bake in a very hot oven, 230°C/450°F/Gas 8, for 10 minutes or until the pastry is well risen and brown.

Reduce to moderate, 180°C/350°F/Gas 4, and continue baking for 20 – 25 minutes. Cover loosely with greaseproof paper if the pastry browns too much.

PUFF PASTRY

Makes 450 g/1 lb (approx)

225 g/8 oz plain flour

1/2 × 2.5 ml spoon/1/4 teaspoon salt

225 g/8 oz butter

1 × 2.5 ml spoon/1/2 teaspoon lemon juice

cold water

Sift together the flour and salt into a bowl and rub in 50 g/2 oz of the butter. Add the lemon juice to the flour and mix to a smooth dough with cold water. Shape the remaining butter into a rectangle on greaseproof paper. Roll out the dough on a lightly floured surface into a strip a little wider than the butter and rather more than twice its length. Place the butter on one half of the pastry, fold the other half over it, and press the edges together with the rolling-pin. Leave in a cool place for 15 minutes to allow the butter to harden. Roll out into a long strip. Fold the bottom third up and the top third down, press the edges together with the rolling-pin, and turn the pastry so that the folded edges are on the right and left. Roll and fold again, cover and leave in a cool place for 15 minutes. Repeat this process until the pastry has been rolled out six times. Finally, roll out as required and leave in a cool place for 20 minutes before cooking.

Toad in the Hole

TOAD IN THE HOLE

Jackie has always liked anything made with sausages

Serves 4

450 g/1 lb chipolata sausages

BATTER

75 g/3 oz plain flour, sifted

1 x 5 ml spoon/1 teaspoon salt

2 eggs

½ – 1 x 5 ml spoon/½ – 1 teaspoon prepared mustard

300 ml/½ pint milk

100 g/4 oz hard cheese, grated

Prepare the batter first. Mix the flour and salt in a mixing bowl. Make a well in the centre and drop in the eggs and mustard. Gradually mix into a smooth batter, adding the milk, a little at a time. Put to one side.
Grill or fry the sausages until lightly brown. Meanwhile, grease four individual shallow tins, and heat in a hot oven, 220°C/425°F/Gas 7, for 10 minutes.
Whisk the batter until bubbly and stir in half the cheese. Mix well and pour in enough to half-fill each tin. Place the sausages in the centre and scatter over the remaining cheese. Bake for 30 minutes or until well risen and golden-brown. A skewer inserted in the batter will come out clean when it is cooked. Serve immediately, accompanied by a salad.

MY BOILED BACON WITH CIDER

any bacon joint suitable for boiling

cider

sugar

ginger root

4 cloves

6 – 8 black peppercorns

1 bay leaf

2 – 3 juniper berries

GARNISH

raspings

Demerara sugar

A bought or home-cured bacon joint will probably need soaking for 1 – 12 hours before cooking, depending on the saltiness of the meat. Packaged and similar joints do not need soaking as a rule. They can be put into a pan, covered with boiling water, then drained.
Weigh the joint and measure its thickness. Calculate the cooking time according to the thickness of the joint. As a guide, allow 30 minutes for each 450 g/1 lb meat plus 30 minutes extra for any joint more than 10 cm/4 inches thick, eg cook a 900 g/2 lb joint for 1½ hours. Do not undercook the meat, but on no account cook it fast or it will shrink and be tough.
Scrape the underside and rind before boiling any bacon joint. Choose a pan large enough to hold the meat comfortably with a little space to spare, especially if boiling more than one joint at a time. Add enough cold, fresh water and cider to cover the meat. Add the sugar and ginger root. Tie the cloves in a square of muslin with the peppercorns, bay leaf and juniper berries and add to the pan. Heat to simmering point, then simmer steadily for the calculated time. Test for tenderness by piercing the meat, near the bone if it has one, with a skewer.
Alternatively, shorten the cooking time by 15 minutes, and let the meat lie in the hot cooking liquid, off the heat, for 30 minutes. This gives an easier, firmer joint to carve.
Lift out the joint, pat dry, place it on a board and remove the rind. It should come off easily, in one piece. Coat the skinned area thoroughly with raspings, mixed with a little Demerara sugar. Serve hot or cold.

PAT AND JACK'S FAVOURITE SUNDAY ROAST

a joint of pork on the bone suitable for roasting

salt and pepper

oil *or* fat for basting

apricot jam

Ask the butcher to score the rind in narrow lines, or do it yourself with a sharp knife. Weigh the joint to calculate the cooking time, allowing 25 – 30 minutes for each 450 g/1 lb plus 25 – 30 minutes extra. Place the joint on a rack in a shallow roasting tin. Season the meat with salt and pepper and pour over a little oil or rub it with a little fat. Rub some salt into the scored rind to produce crisp crackling. Place the roasting tin in the oven, and cook in a very hot oven, 230°C/450°F/Gas 8 for 10 minutes, then in a fairly hot oven, 190°C/375°F/Gas 5 for the rest of the time. Brush the joint with apricot jam 10 minutes before the end of the cooking time to give a sweet, crisp crackling.
Transfer the cooked meat to a warmed meat dish and keep hot. Prepare the gravy from the sediment in the roasting tin.
Serve with Sage and Onion Stuffing and Apple Sauce.

APPLE SAUCE

Makes 300 ml/¹/₂ pint (approx)

450 g/1 lb apples, peeled, cored and sliced

2 x 15 ml spoons/2 tablespoons water

15 g/¹/₂ oz butter

rind and juice of ¹/₂ lemon

sugar

Put the apples into a saucepan with the water, butter and lemon rind. Cover, and cook over low heat until the apples are reduced to a pulp. Beat until smooth, then rub through a sieve, or process in a blender. Re-heat the sauce with the lemon juice and sugar to taste. Serve hot or cold.

SAGE AND ONION STUFFING

Makes 175 g/6 oz (approx)

4 young sage leaves *or* 1 x 2.5 ml spoon/¹/₂ teaspoon dried sage

2 small onions, parboiled and finely chopped

100 g/4 oz soft white breadcrumbs

50 g/2 oz butter *or* margarine, melted

salt and pepper

Scald the fresh sage leaves, if used, and chop them finely. Mix together with the onions and breadcrumbs. Add the fat, and season to taste. Mix together thoroughly. Use as required.

Sunday lunch with Pat, Jack and Jackie is a real treat

Dolly's Pork Chops with Peaches

DOLLY'S PORK CHOPS WITH PEACHES

Serves 6

6 pork chops
ground pepper
dried sage
1 x 15 ml spoon/1 tablespoon oil
25 g/1 oz butter
6 canned peach halves, drained
salt
1 x 15 ml spoon/1 tablespoon plain flour
300 ml/½ pint basic stock (see page 13)

GARNISH

mustard and cress

Sprinkle each chop with pepper and sage. Heat the oil in a frying pan. Add the chops, and fry until sealed and browned on the underside. Turn with a palette knife and continue to fry until the other side is browned. Reduce the heat and continue to fry, turning once or twice, until the meat is cooked through. The total frying time is 15 – 20 minutes, or longer for thick chops. Arrange on a warmed serving dish, sprinkle with salt and keep hot. Pour the fat from the pan, reserving the sediment.

Melt the butter and add the peach halves. Fry gently until golden on both sides. Top each chop with a peach half, cut side down. Garnish with mustard and cress.

Stir the flour into the reserved sediment and cook. Gradually add the stock and stir until boiling. Season to taste. Serve the gravy separately in a sauce-boat.

RAISED VEAL, PORK AND EGG PIE

Joe likes to have this as part of a Ploughman's

Serves 6

25 g/1 oz plain flour
1½ x 5ml spoons/1½ teaspoons salt
½ x 2.5 ml spoon/¼ teaspoon ground pepper
450 g/1 lb pie veal, cut into small pieces
450 g/1 lb lean pork, cut into small pieces
3 hard-boiled eggs
2 x 15 ml spoons/2 tablespoons water
beaten egg for glazing
150 ml/¼ pint (approx) well-flavoured, cooled and jellied stock

HOT WATER CRUST PASTRY

450 g/1 lb plain flour
1 x 5 ml spoon/1 teaspoon salt
175 g/6 oz lard
250 ml/8 fl oz milk *or* water

Prepare the pastry first. Sift the flour and salt into a warm bowl, make a well in the centre, and keep the bowl in a warm place. Meanwhile, heat together the lard and milk or water until boiling, then add them to the flour, mixing well with a wooden spoon until the pastry is cool enough to knead with the hands. Knead thoroughly, and mould as follows: Reserve one-quarter of the pastry for the lid and leave in the bowl in a warm place, covered with a greased polythene bag. Roll out the remainder to about 5 mm/¼ inch thick, in a round or oval shape. Line a 20 cm/8 inch pie mould with the pastry, taking care not to pull the pastry and making sure that the sides and base are of an even thickness. Leave to cool.

Meanwhile, season the flour with salt and pepper, and toss the pieces of meat in it. Put half the meat into the cooled pastry case and put in the whole eggs. Add the rest of the meat and the water. Roll out the pastry reserved for the lid, dampen the rim of the case, put on the lid, brush with beaten egg, and make a hole in the centre to allow steam to escape. Bake in a very hot oven, 230°C/450°F/Gas 8, for 15 minutes. Reduce the heat to very cool, 140°C/275°F/Gas 1, and continue cooking for 2½ hours. Remove the mould for the last 30 minutes of the cooking time and brush the top and sides of the pastry with beaten egg.

Heat the stock until melted and, when the pie is cooked, funnel it through the hole in the lid until the pie is full. Cool completely before serving.

BUBBLE AND SQUEAK

Jackie always enjoys this, Winter and Summer

dripping *or* lard
thin slices of cold roast, braised *or* boiled meat as available
1 medium-sized onion, thinly sliced
cold mashed potatoes as available
cold, cooked green vegetables of any kind, as available
salt and pepper
a dash of vinegar

Heat just enough dripping or lard in a frying pan to cover the bottom. Put in the meat, and fry quickly on both sides until lightly browned. Remove, and keep hot.

Fry the onion until lightly browned, adding a little more fat to the frying pan if necessary. Mix together the potatoes and green vegetables, season to taste, and add to the frying pan. Stir until thoroughly hot, then add a little vinegar. Allow to become slightly crusty on the bottom.

Turn the vegetables on to a warmed dish, place the meat on top, and serve.

Matt and Jackie both love good traditional cooking

EMMERDALE PASTIES

Makes 8

100 g/4 oz raw meat, minced
100 g/4 oz potato, cut into 1.25 cm/½ inch cubes
50 g/2 oz onion, finely chopped
dried mixed herbs
salt and pepper
2 × 15 ml spoons/2 tablespoons gravy *or* water
350 g/12 oz prepared shortcrust pastry
milk for glazing

Mix together the meat and potato. Add the onion with the herbs, seasoning and gravy or water. Roll out the pastry 5 mm/¼ inch thick on a lightly floured surface, and cut it into eight 12.5 cm/5 inch rounds. Divide the filling between the rounds, making a mound in the centre of each. Moisten the edges of the pastry, then lift them to meet over the filling. Pinch and flute the edges to seal. Prick the pasties with a fork and brush them with milk. Bake in a hot oven, 220°C/425°F/Gas 7, for 10 minutes, then reduce to moderate, 180°C/350°F/Gas 4, and bake for a further 50 minutes. Serve hot or cold.

Emmerdale Pasties

SHORTCRUST PASTRY

Makes 350 g/12 oz (approx)

225 g/8 oz plain flour
1 × 2.5 ml spoon/½ teaspoon salt
50 g/2 oz lard
50 g/2 oz butter *or* margarine
3 × 15 ml spoons/3 tablespoons cold water

Sift together the flour and salt into a bowl. Rub the fats into the flour until the mixture resembles fine breadcrumbs. Mix to a stiff dough with cold water. Roll out on a lightly floured surface, and use as required.

Poultry and Game

CHICKEN CASSEROLE

Another of Joe's favourites

Serves 6

25 g/1 oz flour
salt and pepper
1 chicken, jointed *or* 6 small chicken joints
50 g/2 oz butter
125 g/5 oz streaky bacon, without rinds and cut into strips 1.25 cm/½ inch wide
50 g/2 oz mushrooms, sliced
25 g/1 oz shallots, chopped
600 ml/1 pint chicken stock

Season the flour with salt and pepper and dip the joints in it. Melt the butter in a flameproof casserole and gently fry the bacon, mushrooms and shallots. Add the chicken joints and fry until golden on all sides, turning them as required. Add enough hot stock just to cover the chicken pieces, then simmer for 1 – 1½ hours or until tender. Re-season if required. Serve from the casserole.

PAT'S CHICKEN VOL-AU-VENT

Serves 4

175 g/6 oz cooked chicken meat, diced

50 g/2 oz cooked ham, diced

50 g/2 oz button mushrooms, thinly sliced

a pinch of grated nutmeg

salt and pepper

one baked 15 cm/6 inch vol-au-vent case

mustard and cress

BÉCHAMEL SAUCE

$^1/_2$ small onion

$^1/_2$ small carrot

a piece of celery

300 ml/$^1/_2$ pint milk

$^1/_2$ bay leaf

a few parsley stalks

$^1/_2$ sprig thyme

salt

$^1/_2$ clove

3 white peppercorns

$^1/_2$ blade of mace

25 g/1 oz butter

25 g/1 oz flour

2 x 15 ml spoons/2 tablespoons single cream

Make the Béchamel sauce first. Heat the vegetables gently to simmering point with the milk, herbs, salt and spices. Cover and leave to infuse for 30 minutes. Do not allow to boil. Strain the milk. Melt the butter in a saucepan, add the flour, and stir until smooth. Cook over gentle heat, without allowing it to colour, for 2 – 3 minutes, stirring until the mixture begins to bubble. Draw the pan off the heat, and gradually add the flavoured milk, stirring to prevent lumps forming. Return to moderate heat and bring the sauce to the boil, stirring all the time. When the sauce has thickened, simmer for 3 – 4 minutes, beating briskly. Re-season if required. Add the cream to the sauce just at boiling point, and remove from the heat immediately.

Add the meat and mushrooms to the Béchamel sauce, and heat thoroughly, stirring all the time. Add the nutmeg and seasoning. Meanwhile, re-heat the vol-au-vent case in a warm oven, 160°C/325°F/Gas 3, for 10 minutes. Fill with the hot mixture, and serve at once, garnished with mustard and cress.

PAT'S SPECIAL ROAST CHICKEN

A recipe handed down by her mother

Serves 4 – 6

oil *or* fat for basting

1 x 2.25 kg/5 lb roasting chicken, trussed

salt and pepper

2 – 3 rashers streaky bacon

1 x 15 ml spoon/1 tablespoon plain flour

300 ml/$^1/_2$ pint chicken stock

gravy browning

Put the oil or fat in a roasting tin and place for a few minutes in a fairly hot oven, 190°C – 200°C/375°F – 400°F/Gas 5 – 6. Remove from the oven. Place the chicken in the roasting tin, on a trivet if liked. Baste with the fat, sprinkle with salt and pepper, and place the bacon rashers over the breast. Cover the breast with a piece of foil or buttered greaseproof paper, if liked. Return the tin to the oven and cook the bird in a warm oven, 160°C/325°F/Gas 3, for 2$^1/_2$ – 3 hours until tender. The bacon and foil or greaseproof paper should be removed 10 – 15 minutes before serving, to allow the breast to brown.

When cooked, place the chicken on a hot carving dish, remove the trussing strings or skewers, and keep hot. Pour out and discard the excess fat from the tin, keeping back the sediment for gravy. Sprinkle in the flour, stir well and add the stock gradually. Bring to the boil and boil for 2 – 3 minutes. Season to taste, add a little gravy browning, and strain into a hot sauce-boat. Serve with bacon rolls and Bread Sauce (page 51).

BREAD SAUCE

Makes 300 ml/¹/₂ pint (approx)

300 ml/¹/₂ pint milk
2 cloves
a blade of mace
4 peppercorns
1 allspice berry
1 bay leaf
1 large onion, skinned
50 g/2 oz dried white breadcrumbs
1 x 15 ml spoon/1 tablespoon softened butter
salt and pepper
2 x 15 ml spoons/2 tablespoons single cream (optional)

Heat the milk very slowly to boiling point with the spices, bay leaf and onion. Cover the pan and infuse over gentle heat for 30 minutes. Strain the liquid. Add the breadcrumbs and butter to the flavoured milk, then season to taste. Heat the mixture to just below simmering point and keep at this temperature for 20 minutes. Stir in the cream, if used.

DOLLY'S OWN CHICKEN SALAD

Serves 4

1 hard-boiled egg
350 g/12 oz cold cooked chicken, cut into neat pieces
2 sticks celery, chopped
1 x 15 ml spoon/1 tablespoon corn salad oil
1 x 15 ml spoon/1 tablespoon vinegar
salt and pepper
6 x 15 ml spoons/6 tablespoons mayonnaise
lettuce leaves

GARNISH

selection of gherkins, capers, anchovy fillets, radishes and watercress

Chop the egg white. Mix together with the chicken, celery, corn oil, vinegar and seasoning, then leave to stand for 1 hour.
Stir the mayonnaise into the salad. Sieve the egg yolk. Pile the chicken, celery and egg white on to a bed of lettuce, sprinkle with the sieved yolk, and garnish as liked. Chill before serving.

TURKEY FRITTERS

Dolly makes these specially for Matt

Serves 4

50 g/2 oz ham, finely minced
50 g/2 oz soft white breadcrumbs
2 x 5 ml spoons/2 teaspoons chopped parsley
450 g/1 lb sliced cold turkey, cut into neat pieces
1 egg, beaten
oil *or* fat for deep frying

Mix together the ham, breadcrumbs and parsley. Dip the turkey in the beaten egg and coat with the breadcrumb mixture. Press the coating on firmly. Fry the fritters in deep fat, then drain and serve immediately.

Pat enjoys cooking both traditional and more unusual recipes

MY CHICKEN PIE

Dad likes this hot or cold

Serves 6 – 8

1 chicken with giblets
300 ml/1 pint water
1 onion
salt and pepper
bouquet garni
a blade of whole mace
1 x 2.5 ml spoon/$\frac{1}{2}$ teaspoon grated nutmeg
1 x 2.5 ml spoon/$\frac{1}{2}$ teaspoon ground mace
6 slices lean cooked ham
175 g/6 oz herb forcemeat
3 hard-boiled eggs, sliced
150 ml/$\frac{1}{4}$ pint water
flour for dredging
425 g/15 oz prepared puff pastry (see page 44)
beaten egg for glazing

Skin the chicken and cut it into small serving joints. Put the leftover bones, neck and gizzard into a small pan with the water. Split the onion in half and add it to the pan with the seasoning, bouquet garni and mace. Half cover and simmer gently for about 45 minutes until the liquid is well reduced and strongly flavoured. Put to one side.

Put a layer of chicken joints in the bottom of a lightly greased 1.8 litre/3 pint pie dish. Season lightly with salt, pepper, nutmeg and ground mace. Cover with a layer of ham, then with forcemeat; re-season to taste. Place a layer of eggs over the forcemeat, and season again. Repeat the layers until the dish is full and all the ingredients are used, ending with a layer of chicken joints. Pour the water into the dish and dredge lightly with flour.

Roll out the pastry on a lightly floured surface and use to cover the dish. Trim the edge, knock up and flute the edge. Make a small hole in the centre of the lid, and decorate round with pastry leaves. Make a pastry rose to cover the hole after baking. Brush the pastry with the beaten egg.

Bake the pie in a hot oven, 220°C/425°F/Gas 7, for 15 minutes to set the pastry, then reduce the temperature to moderate, 180°C/350°F/Gas 4, and cover the pastry loosely with greaseproof paper. Bake for 1$\frac{1}{2}$ – 2 hours. Bake the pastry rose blind.

Test whether the joints are cooked through by running a small heated skewer into the pie through the central hole. It should come out clean with no trace of blood or smell of raw meat on it.

Just before the pie is cooked, re-heat the stock and strain it. When the pie is cooked, funnel the stock through the hole in the pastry, and cover with the pastry rose. Serve hot or cold.

HERB FORCEMEAT

Makes 175 g/6 oz (approx)

100 g/4 oz soft breadcrumbs
50 g/2 oz shredded suet
a pinch of grated nutmeg
1 x 15 ml spoon/1 tablespoon chopped parsley
1 x 5 ml spoon/1 teaspoon chopped fresh mixed herbs
grated rind of $\frac{1}{2}$ lemon
salt and pepper
1 egg, beaten

Mix the breadcrumbs with the suet, then add the nutmeg, herbs and lemon rind. Season to taste, then stir in the egg to bind the mixture. Use as required.

HERB FORCEMEAT BALLS

basic herb forcemeat mixture

Form the mixture into balls, and bake in a moderate oven, 180°C/350°F/Gas 4, for 15 – 20 minutes, or fry in deep or shallow fat until golden.

GROUSE PIE

Seth never says 'No' to a cooked game dish

Serves 6 – 8

350 g/12 oz rump steak, thinly sliced
2 hard-boiled eggs, sliced
salt and pepper
2 grouse, jointed (reserve the necks and trimmings)
2 – 3 rashers bacon, without rinds and cut into strips
300 ml/½ pint basic stock (see page 13)
225 g/8 oz prepared puff pastry (see page 44)
beaten egg *or* milk for glazing

Season the steak and eggs to taste. Line the bottom of a 1.2 litre/2 pint pie dish with some of the pieces of seasoned steak, cover with a layer of grouse, and pack round them some bacon, egg and seasoning. Repeat the layers until the dish is full. Add enough stock to fill three-quarters of the pie dish.

Roll out the pastry on a lightly floured surface and use to cover the dish. Trim the edge, knock up and flute the edge. Make a small hole in the centre of the lid, and decorate round with the trimmings.

Bake the pie in a hot oven, 220°C/425°F/Gas 7, for 20 minutes, then lower the heat to moderate, 180°C/350°F/Gas 4, and cook for another 1¼ – 1½ hours. Glaze the pastry with the egg or milk 30 minutes before the cooking is complete.

Meanwhile, simmer the reserved necks and trimmings of the birds in the remaining stock, then strain and season. Funnel the hot stock through the hole in the pastry just before serving.

PHEASANT PILAF

Enjoyed by Jack and Seth

Serves 4

75 g/3 oz dried apricots
75 g/3 oz prunes
225 g/8 oz long-grain rice
50 g/2 oz butter
75 g/3 oz blanched almonds
75 g/3 oz seedless raisins
1 cold roasted pheasant, boned and diced
2 eggs, beaten
2 × 15 ml spoons/2 tablespoons clear honey
2 × 15 ml spoons/2 tablespoons chopped parsley
salt and pepper

Soak the apricots and prunes overnight. Stone the prunes. Cook the rice in boiling salted water for 12 – 15 minutes until tender, then drain well. Melt the butter in a frying pan and brown the almonds lightly. Drain and add the soaked fruits and raisins. Add the pheasant meat and heat through for 5 minutes. Add the eggs with the cooked rice and all the remaining ingredients. Cook, stirring frequently, until the eggs are lightly set. Serve at once.

Seth can be relied on to provide quality game

Fresh From the Garden

PAT'S VEGETABLE CASSEROLE

Serves 4 – 6

2 x 15 ml spoons/2 tablespoons oil
450 g/1 lb onions, chopped
2 cloves garlic, crushed
2 green peppers, chopped
450 g/1 lb courgettes, sliced
2 medium-sized aubergines, sliced
450 g/1 lb tomatoes, sliced
225 g/8 oz mushrooms
75 g/3 oz concentrated tomato purée
2 bay leaves
1 x 15 ml spoon/1 tablespoon chopped parsley
1 x 5 ml spoon/1 teaspoon chopped marjoram
1 x 5 ml spoon/1 teaspoon chopped thyme
salt and pepper
300 ml/½ pint vegetable stock *or* water
450 g/1 lb potatoes, thinly sliced
25 g/1 oz butter

Heat the oil in a frying pan and fry the onions, garlic and peppers for 5 minutes. Turn into a casserole with the courgettes, aubergines, tomatoes, mushrooms, tomato purée, herbs and seasoning. Mix well and pour in the stock or water. Arrange the potatoes on the top, dot with the butter, and cover. Cook in a moderate oven, 180°C/350°F/Gas 4, for 1 hour, then remove the lid and cook for a further 30 minutes or until the potatoes are golden-brown.

VEGETABLE STOCK

Makes 2.4 litres/4 pints (approx)

25 g/1 oz butter *or* margarine
2 large carrots, thinly sliced
2 medium-sized onions, thinly sliced
3 sticks celery, thinly sliced
2 tomatoes, chopped
2.4 litres/4 pints boiling water
1 x 2.5 ml spoon/½ teaspoon yeast extract
bouquet garni
1 x 5 ml spoon/1 teaspoon salt
6 black peppercorns
a blade of mace
outer leaves of 1 lettuce, shredded

Melt the fat in a large saucepan and fry the carrots, onions and celery for 5 – 10 minutes until the onions are golden-brown. Add the tomatoes and fry for a further minute. Add the water and the rest of the ingredients, except the lettuce. Cover and simmer for 1 hour. Add the lettuce to the pan, then simmer for a further 20 minutes. Strain through a fine sieve. Use the same day, if possible, or cool quickly and store in a refrigerator for up to 2 days.

Henry's special Cauliflower Cheese

HENRY'S SPECIAL CAULIFLOWER CHEESE

Serves 4

1 medium-sized firm cauliflower
2 x 15 ml spoons/2 tablespoons butter *or* margarine
4 x 15 ml spoons/4 tablespoons flour
250 ml/8 fl oz milk
125 g/5 oz grated Cheddar cheese
a pinch of dry mustard
a pinch of Cayenne pepper
salt and pepper
25 g/1 oz fine dry white breadcrumbs

Put the cauliflower in a saucepan containing enough boiling salted water to half-cover it. Cover the pan, and cook gently for 20 – 30 minutes until tender. Drain well, reserving 150 ml/¼ pint of the cooking water. Break the head carefully into sections, and place in a warmed ovenproof dish. Keep warm under greased greaseproof paper.

Melt the fat in a medium-sized pan, stir in the flour, and cook for 2 – 3 minutes, stirring all the time, without letting the flour colour. Mix together the milk and reserved cooking water, and gradually add to the pan, stirring all the time to prevent lumps forming. Bring the sauce to the boil, lower the heat, and simmer until thickened. Remove from the heat, and stir in 100 g/4 oz of the cheese, with the mustard and Cayenne pepper. Season to taste. Stir until the cheese is fully melted, then pour the sauce over the cauliflower. Mix the remaining cheese with the breadcrumbs, and sprinkle them on top. Place in a hot oven, 220°C/425°F/Gas 7, for 7 – 10 minutes, to brown the top. Serve at once.

STUFFED ONIONS

All the family have always enjoyed these

Serves 6

6 large onions
75 g/3 oz cooked meat, chopped *or* minced
2 x 15 ml spoons/2 tablespoons soft white breadcrumbs
1 x 2.5 ml spoon/½ teaspoon finely chopped sage
salt and pepper
beaten egg
2 x 10 ml spoons/2 dessertspoons butter *or* margarine

Parboil the onions in their skins for 45 minutes or until almost tender. Drain, skin, and remove the centres with a teaspoon. Chop the onion centres finely. Add the meat to the chopped onion with the breadcrumbs, sage and seasoning. Bind the stuffing together with enough beaten egg to give a fairly firm mixture. Divide between the hollows in the onions. (A band of stiff paper can be tied round each onion to prevent it splitting, but this is not essential.) Dot the tops of the onions with the fat and cook, uncovered, in a moderate oven, 180°C/350°F/Gas 4, for 45 minutes, or until tender. Serve with Tomato Sauce.

TOMATO SAUCE

Makes 600 ml/1 pint (approx)

2 x 15 ml spoons/2 tablespoons olive oil
1 medium-sized onion, finely chopped
1 clove of garlic, crushed
1 rasher of streaky bacon, without rinds and chopped
675 g/1½ lb tomatoes, skinned, de-seeded and chopped
salt and pepper
a pinch of sugar
1 x 5 ml spoon/1 teaspoon chopped fresh basil

Heat the oil in a saucepan, and fry the onion, garlic and bacon for 5 minutes. Add the other ingredients, cover and simmer gently for 30 minutes. Rub through a sieve or process in a blender until smooth. Re-heat and re-season if required.

TOMATO AND ONION PIE

Dad grows the vegetables and I cook them

Serves 4

450 g/1 lb large onions, skinned
50 g/2 oz butter
900 g/2 lb tomatoes, skinned and sliced
salt and pepper
50 g/2 oz Cheddar cheese, grated
50 g/2 oz soft white breadcrumbs

Put the onions into a bowl, and cover with boiling water. Leave for 5 minutes, drain, dry thoroughly, and cut into slices. Melt half the butter in a pan and fry the onions until golden-brown. Place them in alternate layers with the tomatoes in a greased pie dish, sprinkle each layer lightly with salt and pepper and liberally with cheese and some of the breadcrumbs. Cover the whole with the remaining breadcrumbs and dot with the remaining butter. Cook in a fairly hot oven, 190°C/375°F/Gas 5, for 45 minutes.

MY GRANDMOTHER'S PEASE PUDDING

Serves 6

550 g/1¼ lb split peas
1 small onion, skinned
bouquet garni
salt and pepper
50 g/2 oz butter *or* margarine, cut into small pieces
2 eggs, beaten

Soak the peas overnight. Drain, put into a pan, and cover with fresh cold water. Add the onion to the pan with the bouquet garni and seasoning. Cover and simmer the peas slowly for about 2 – 2½ hours or until tender. Drain thoroughly, then sieve to form a purée. Add the butter and eggs to the pea purée with the seasoning. Beat well together. Place the mixture in a floured cloth and tie tightly. Simmer gently in boiling, salted water for 1 hour. Remove from the pan, take out of the cloth, and serve very hot.
Serve with sausages or pickled pork.

MY MIXED VEGETABLE SALAD

Grown in our own garden

Serves 4 – 6

| 3 large new potatoes |
| 3 young turnips |
| ½ bunch young carrots |
| 225 g/8 oz shelled peas |
| 1 x 15 ml spoon/1 tablespoon chopped parsley |
| 1 x 5 ml spoon/1 teaspoon chopped mint |
| 150 ml/¼ pint mayonnaise |
| salt and pepper |
| a pinch of paprika |

Boil or steam the potatoes, turnips and carrots in their skins. Drain thoroughly, then peel and dice neatly. Boil or steam the peas. Add to the remaining vegetables with the parsley, mint, mayonnaise and seasoning, and mix well. Turn into a serving dish and sprinkle with a little paprika before serving.

My Mushroom and Cucumber Salad

SUMMER SALAD

Nothing better on a hot day, particularly when grown by Dad!

Serves 6

| 1 large lettuce |
| ½ small cucumber, thinly sliced |
| 3 tomatoes, sliced |
| ½ bunch radishes, sliced |

GARNISH

| 2 hard-boiled eggs, thickly sliced |
| watercress sprigs |

Reserve the best lettuce leaves and shred the remaining ones. Mix with half the cucumber, tomatoes and radishes.
Line a salad bowl with the reserved lettuce leaves and pile the salad into the centre. Garnish with the reserved cucumber, tomatoes and radishes, the eggs and the watercress.
Serve with whole spring onions and a salad dressing.

MY MUSHROOM AND CUCUMBER SALAD

Another of Jack's favourites

Serves 4

| ¼ Webbs lettuce, finely shredded |
| 100 g/4 oz button mushrooms, cut into quarters |
| ½ cucumber, diced |

DRESSING

| 4 x 15 ml spoons/4 tablespoons mayonnaise |
| 2 x 5 ml spoons/2 teaspoons tomato ketchup |
| 1 x 2.5 ml spoon/½ teaspoon lemon juice |

GARNISH

| a pinch of paprika |

Divide the lettuce between four salad bowls. Mix together the mushrooms and cucumber, and place on top of the lettuce.
Mix together thoroughly the mayonnaise, tomato ketchup and lemon juice and pour this over the mushrooms. Sprinkle with a little paprika.

Pat's Tomato and Onion Salad and Special Coleslaw and My own Green Salad

MY OWN GREEN SALAD

Serves 4

1 clove of garlic, halved

1 Webbs, Cos *or* round lettuce

French dressing

Press the cut sides of the garlic against the base and sides of a salad bowl. Tear the lettuce into small pieces and put into the bowl. Just before serving, pour the dressing over the salad, and toss the lettuce until every piece is coated.

PAT'S TOMATO AND ONION SALAD

Serves 4

450 g/1 lb tomatoes, skinned and sliced very thinly

French dressing

1 x 5 ml spoon/1 teaspoon finely chopped onion

1 x 15 ml spoon/1 tablespoon finely chopped parsley

Arrange the sliced tomatoes in a large shallow serving dish. Pour over the dressing and sprinkle with the onion and parsley. Serve chilled.

PAT'S SPECIAL COLESLAW

Serves 4

1 small *or* medium-sized head of white cabbage, shredded *or* finely grated
2 eating apples, peeled and coarsely grated
1 x 15 ml spoon/1 tablespoon finely grated onion
2 x 15 ml spoons/2 tablespoons finely chopped parsley
50 g/2 oz Leicester cheese, grated

DRESSING

150 ml/¼ pint soured cream
2 x 15 ml spoons/2 tablespoons milk
1 x 15 ml spoon/1 tablespoon lemon juice
2 x 5 ml spoons/2 teaspoons rose-hip syrup
1 x 2.5 ml spoon/½ teaspoon Worcestershire sauce
1 x 2.5 ml spoon/½ teaspoon salt

Put the cabbage and apples into a large bowl. Add the onion, parsley and cheese, and mix well. Mix together the dressing ingredients, and pour over the cabbage mixture. Toss well, then transfer to a serving dish.

RED CABBAGE SALAD

Amos always asks me for this

Serves 6

3 eating apples, preferably with green skins, thinly sliced
75 ml/3 fl oz French dressing
1 x 5 ml spoon/1 teaspoon prepared mustard
450 g/1 lb red cabbage, finely shredded

GARNISH

mustard and cress

Quickly toss the apples in the dressing to preserve their colour. Add the mustard and mix well, then add the cabbage and toss lightly. Pile into a salad bowl and garnish with cress before serving.

Amos has acquired quite a taste for my salads

DOLLY'S MARINATED CARROT SALAD

Serves 6

675 g/1½ lb young carrots, cut into quarters lengthways
1 x 10 ml spoon/1 dessertspoon French mustard

MARINADE

1 clove of garlic, crushed
150 ml/¼ pint water
150 ml/¼ pint wine vinegar
150 ml/¼ pint white wine
1 x 5 ml spoon/1 teaspoon salt
1 x 5 ml spoon/1 teaspoon sugar
1 sprig of parsley
1 sprig of thyme
1 bay leaf
a good pinch of Cayenne pepper
150 ml/¼ pint olive oil

Make the marinade first. Put the garlic into a pan with the other marinade ingredients. Bring to the boil, add the carrots, and cook gently for 15 minutes or until the carrots are just tender. Drain, reserving the liquor. Place the carrots in a deep serving dish. Strain the cooking liquor, stir in the mustard, and pour this over the carrots. Leave to marinate overnight.

Emmerdale Farm's Favourite Puddings and Desserts

Hot Puddings

APPLE AND BLACKBERRY PUDDING

Dad and I enjoy this very much, particularly as we use our own fruit

Serves 6

225 g/8 oz plain flour
1 x 5 ml spoon/1 teaspoon baking powder
a pinch of salt
75 g/3 oz shredded suet

FILLING

75 g/3 oz granulated sugar
350 g/12 oz cooking apples, peeled, cored and sliced
350 g/12 oz blackberries
2 x 15 ml spoons/2 tablespoons cold water

Sift together the flour, baking powder and salt. Add the suet and enough cold water to make a soft but not sticky dough. Cut off and reserve one-quarter of the pastry for the lid. Use the remaining pastry to line a greased 900 ml/1½ pint basin.

To make the filling, stir the sugar into the apples, then put with the blackberries into the prepared basin and add the cold water. Cover with the reserved pastry and seal well. Cover with a well-floured cloth, greased paper or foil and boil for 2½ – 3 hours. Serve from the basin, or leave for 5 – 10 minutes at room temperature to firm up, then turn out.
Serve with custard.

Dad and I frequently confer on the week's cooking

RHUBARB CRUMBLE

Joe is very fond of this

Serves 6

550 g/1¼ lb rhubarb, sliced
100 g/4 oz brown sugar
50 ml/2 fl oz water
grated rind of 1 lemon
75 g/3 oz butter *or* margarine
175 g/6 oz plain flour
75 g/3 oz caster sugar
½ × 2.5 ml spoon/¼ teaspoon ground ginger

Cook the rhubarb in a covered pan until soft with the sugar, water and lemon rind. Fill a greased 1.2 litre/2 pint pie dish with the rhubarb. Rub the fat into the flour until it resembles fine breadcrumbs. Add the caster sugar and ginger and stir well, then sprinkle the mixture over the rhubarb, and press down lightly. Bake in a moderate oven, 180°C/350°F/Gas 4, for 30 – 40 minutes until the crumble is golden-brown.

BAKED JAM ROLL

Joe, like his father and grandfather before him, loves this

Serves 6

350 g/12 oz plain flour
1 × 5 ml spoon/1 teaspoon baking powder
a pinch of salt
175 g/6 oz shredded suet
225 – 350 g/8 – 12 oz jam

Sift the flour, baking powder and salt into a bowl. Add the suet and enough cold water to make a soft but firm dough. On a lightly floured surface, roll into a rectangle about 5 mm/¼ inch thick. Spread the jam almost to the edges, dampen the edges, and roll up lightly. Seal the edges at each end. Place the roll on a greased baking sheet with the sealed edge underneath. Cover loosely with greased paper or foil, then bake in a fairly hot oven, 190°C/375°F/Gas 5, for 50 – 60 minutes until golden-brown.
Serve on a warm platter, sliced, with warmed jam.

Dolly's Apple Fritters

DOLLY'S APPLE FRITTERS

Cooked specially for Matt

Serves 4

450 g/1 lb apples, peeled and cored and cut into 5 mm/¼ inch slices
water
lemon juice
caster sugar

BATTER

100 g/4 oz plain flour, sifted
½ × 2.5 ml spoon/ ¼ teaspoon salt
1 × 15 ml spoon/1 tablespoon vegetable oil
150 ml/¼ pint water *or* milk and water
2 egg whites

Dry the fruit well, then put into water containing a little lemon juice until needed.
Meanwhile, prepare the batter. Mix the flour with the salt, oil and some of the liquid, then beat well until smooth. Stir in the rest of the liquid. Just before using, whisk the egg whites until stiff and fold into the batter.
Drain the fruit well, then dry with soft kitchen paper. Coat with the batter and fry, turning once, until crisp and golden. Serve hot, sprinkled with caster sugar.

BAKEWELL TART

Serves 4 – 5

200 g/7 oz prepared shortcrust pastry (see page 49)

raspberry jam

50 g/2 oz butter

50 g/2 oz caster sugar

1 egg

25 g/1 oz ground almonds

25 g/1 oz fine plain cake crumbs

a few drops almond essence

icing sugar for dusting

Roll out the pastry on a lightly floured surface and use it to line a 17.5 cm/7 inch flan ring. Spread over it a good layer of the jam. Beat together the butter and sugar until pale and fluffy. Beat in the egg, then add the almonds, cake crumbs and essence. Beat until well mixed, then pour the mixture into the flan shell, over the jam, and bake in a fairly hot oven, 200°C/400°F/Gas 6, for 25 minutes until firm. Sprinkle with icing sugar and serve hot or cold.

EVE'S PUDDING

Serves 4

450 g/1 lb cooking apples, peeled, cored and thinly sliced

grated rind and juice of 1 lemon

75 g/3 oz Demerara sugar

1 x 15 ml spoon/1 tablespoon water

75 g/3 oz butter *or* margarine

75 g/3 oz caster sugar

1 egg, beaten

100 g/4 oz self-raising flour

Mix together the apples with the lemon rind and juice, Demerara sugar and water, and put into a greased 1.2 litre/2 pint pie dish. Cream together the fat and caster sugar until light and fluffy, then beat in the egg. Fold in the flour lightly and spread the mixture over the apples. Bake in a moderate oven, 180°C/350°F/Gas 4, for 40 – 45 minutes until the apples are soft and the sponge is firm.
Serve with melted apple jelly and single cream.

BROWN BREAD PUDDING

Matt often asks me for this when he's at the Farm

Serves 4 – 6

200 g/7 oz stale brown breadcrumbs

75 g/3 oz raisins

75 g/3 oz sultanas

100 g/4 oz shredded suet

75 g/3 oz caster sugar

2 eggs

milk

Mix together all the ingredients, adding enough milk to make a dropping consistency. Leave to stand for 30 minutes. Add more milk if the pudding is too stiff, to give a dropping consistency. Put the mixture into a greased 900 ml/1½ pint basin, cover with greased paper or foil and steam for 2½ – 3 hours. Serve from the basin, or leave for 5 – 10 minutes at room temperature to firm up, then turn out.
Serve with custard.

JAM SPONGE PUDDING

I often make this for Dad

Serves 4 – 6

100 g/4 oz butter *or* margarine

100 g/4 oz caster sugar

2 eggs, beaten

175 g/6 oz plain flour

1 x 5 ml spoon/1 teaspoon baking powder

½ x 2.5 ml spoon/¼ teaspoon vanilla essence

2 x 15 ml spoons/2 tablespoons milk (approx)

2 x 15 ml spoons/2 tablespoons jam

Cream together the fat and sugar until light and fluffy, then gradually beat in the eggs. Sift together the flour and baking powder, and fold them in. Add the essence and enough milk to form a soft dropping consistency. Put the jam in the bottom of a greased 1.2 litre/2 pint pie dish, then cover with the sponge mixture. Bake in a moderate oven, 180°C/350°F/Gas 4, for 30 – 35 minutes until well risen and golden-brown.
Serve from the dish with a jam sauce made with the same jam.

BAKED APPLES

Amos and Henry are very partial to this

Serves 6

6 medium-sized cooking apples, cored
25 g/1 oz flaked almonds
40 g/1½ oz seedless raisins
25 – 50 g/1 – 2 oz boiled rice (preferably boiled in milk)
50 g/2 oz sugar *or* to taste
1 egg, beaten
2 x 15 ml spoons/2 tablespoons butter, melted
blackcurrant syrup

With a small rounded spoon, hollow out part of the apple flesh surrounding the core hole. Do not break the outside skin. Mix together the almonds, raisins and rice, using enough rice to make a stuffing for all the apples. Add the sugar to the rice and nuts, and enough egg to bind the mixture, then add the butter. Fill the apples with the rice mixture. Place in a baking tray, and add 5 mm/¼ inch depth hot water. Bake in a fairly hot oven, 190°C/375°F/Gas 5, for 40 minutes or until the apples are tender, then place on a warmed serving platter. Warm the blackcurrant syrup and pour it over the apples. Serve with chilled cream.

FRUIT ROLY-POLY

Jack still enjoys this, so many years after he left the Farm

Serves 6 – 7

350 g/12 oz plain flour
½ x 2.5 ml spoon/¼ teaspoon salt
2 x 5 ml spoons/2 teaspoons baking powder
175 g/6 oz shredded suet
175 g/6 oz chopped dates

Sift together the dry ingredients. Add the suet, dates and enough cold water to make a soft but not sticky dough. Shape into a roll. Lay the dough on a scalded, well-floured pudding cloth and roll up loosely. Tie up the ends of the cloth. Put into a saucepan of fast-boiling water, reduce the heat and simmer for 2 – 2½ hours. Drain well and unwrap. Serve sliced, with warmed golden syrup and cream.

SYRUP SPONGE PUDDING

Another of Matt's favourites when he's at the Farm

Serves 5

175 g/6 oz butter *or* margarine
175 g/6 oz caster sugar
3 eggs
grated rind of ½ lemon
175 g/6 oz plain flour
1 x 5 ml spoon/1 teaspoon baking powder
2 x 15 ml spoons/2 tablespoons golden syrup

Work together the fat and sugar until light and creamy. Beat in the eggs gradually, then add the lemon rind. Sift together the flour and baking powder and fold lightly into the mixture. Put the syrup into the base of a greased 900 ml/1½ pint basin, then turn in the sponge mixture. Cover with greased paper or foil and steam for 1¼ – 1½ hours. Leave in the basin at room temperature for 3 – 5 minutes, then turn out. Serve with warmed golden syrup.

Syrup Sponge Pudding

PLUM AND WALNUT PIE

Dad loves this in Autumn when he can gather fresh walnuts

Serves 4 – 6

450 g/1 lb golden plums, halved and stoned
100 g/4 oz brown sugar
a pinch of ground cinnamon
grated rind of 1 orange
50 g/2 oz chopped walnuts
225 – 275 g/8 – 10 oz prepared shortcrust pastry (see page 49)
1 egg white, beaten
granulated sugar

Put half the plums into a 600 ml/1 pint pie dish
with the sugar, cinnamon, orange rind and
chopped walnuts. Add the remaining plums.
Roll out the pastry on a lightly floured surface
and use to cover the dish. Trim the edge, knock up
and flute the edge. Brush the top with the beaten
egg white, and sprinkle with the granulated sugar.
Make a small hole in the centre of the pastry, and
bake in a moderate oven, 180°C/350°F/Gas 4, for
about 50 minutes until the pastry is golden-brown.
Serve hot, with double cream.

SANDIE'S JAM TART

Serves 6

300 g/11 oz prepared shortcrust pastry (see page 49)
4 – 6 x 15 ml spoons/4 – 6 tablespoons any firm jam
beaten egg *or* milk for glazing

Roll out the pastry on a lightly floured surface and
use it to line a 20 cm/8 inch pie plate. Decorate the
edge with any trimmings. Fill with jam, and glaze
the uncovered pastry with beaten egg or milk. Bake
in a hot oven, 220°/425°F/Gas 7, for about
15 minutes or until the pastry is cooked, covering
with greaseproof paper if a very firm jam is used.
Serve hot or cold.

Plum and Walnut Pie

Pat's Orange Soufflé

PAT'S ORANGE SOUFFLÉ

Serves 4

2 oranges
75 g/3 oz caster sugar
300 ml/¹/₂ pint milk
75 g/3 oz butter
50 g/2 oz plain flour
4 eggs, separated
icing sugar

Finely grate the rind of both oranges. Squeeze the juice of one and put to one side. Add the sugar and grated rind to the milk, heat gently to boiling point, then turn off the heat. Leave to infuse for 5 – 7 minutes.

Melt the butter in a saucepan, stir in the flour and cook slowly for 2 minutes without allowing the flour to colour; stir all the time. Add the flavoured milk gradually, stirring constantly, and beat until smooth. Bring the sauce to the boil and add the reserved orange juice. Remove from the heat. Add the yolks to the sauce, one by one, beating well together. Whisk the whites until fairly stiff. Stir 1 x 15 ml spoon/1 tablespoon into the sauce, then fold in the remainder. Turn at once into a buttered 1.2 litre/2 pint soufflé dish and bake in a preheated fairly hot oven, 190°C/375°F/Gas 5, for about 35 – 40 minutes until risen and browned. Sprinkle with a little icing sugar, and serve at once with chilled pouring cream.

FLOATING ISLANDS

Serves 4

3 eggs, separated
225 g/8 oz caster sugar
600 ml/1 pint milk
a few drops vanilla essence

Whisk the egg whites until very stiff, then fold in 175 g/6 oz caster sugar.

Pour the milk into a frying pan and add a few drops of vanilla essence. Heat gently until the surface of the milk is just shivering. It must not boil or the milk will discolour and form a skin.

Using two dessertspoons, mould egg shapes from the meringue and slide them into the milk. Make only a few at a time, and leave plenty of space between them in the pan as they swell when cooking. Cook slowly for 5 minutes, then turn them over, using a palette knife and a spoon, and cook for a further 5 minutes. They are very delicate and must be handled with care. Remove from the milk gently and place on a cloth or soft kitchen paper to drain. Continue making shapes from the meringue and poaching them in the milk, until all the meringue is used. Arrange the 'islands' in a flat serving dish.

Blend the egg yolks with the rest of the sugar, then stir in the milk gradually. Strain the mixture into a saucepan and cook gently, stirring all the time, until the sauce thickens slightly. Do not let it come near the boil or it will curdle. Pour the custard round the 'islands' and serve at once.

QUEEN OF PUDDINGS

A special treat for Jackie

Serves 4

75 g/3 oz soft white breadcrumbs
450 ml/³/₄ pint milk
25 g/1 oz butter
2 x 5 ml spoons/2 teaspoons grated lemon rind
75 g/3 oz caster sugar
2 eggs, separated
2 x 15 ml spoons/2 tablespoons red jam

Dry the breadcrumbs slightly by placing them in a cool oven for a few moments. Warm the milk with the butter and lemon rind to approximately 65°C/149°F; do not let it come near the boil. Stir 25 g/1 oz of the sugar into the yolks, then pour the warmed milk over the yolks, and stir in well. Add the crumbs and mix thoroughly. Pour the custard mixture into a greased 900 ml/1¹/₂ pint pie dish and leave to stand for 30 minutes. Bake in a warm oven, 160°C/325°F/Gas 3, for 40 – 45 minutes until the pudding is lightly set.

Remove the pudding from the oven and reduce the temperature to very cool, 120°C/250°F/Gas ¹/₂. Warm the jam and spread it over the pudding. Whisk the egg whites until stiff, add half the remaining sugar and whisk again. Fold in the remaining sugar, then spoon the meringue over the pudding. Return to the oven for 40 – 45 minutes or until the meringue is set.

Queen of Puddings

My special Treacle Tart

MY SPECIAL TREACLE TART

Serves 6

300 g/11 oz prepared shortcrust pastry (see page 49)

1 Bramley apple, peeled, cored and chopped

150 g/5 oz golden syrup

25 g/1 oz black treacle

50 g/2 oz white breadcrumbs

50 g/2 oz dried mixed fruit

1 x 15 ml spoon/1 tablespoon lemon juice

Roll out the pastry thinly on a lightly floured surface and use it to line a 20 cm/8 inch pie plate. Trim, knock up and flute the edges, reserving the pastry trimmings. Prick the base of the pastry and cover with the chopped apple. Warm the syrup and treacle, mix in the breadcrumbs, dried fruit and lemon juice, and spread over the apple.

Roll out the pastry trimmings and cut off three narrow strips. Twist the strips, one at a time, and place them across the tart filling in a wheel pattern. Dampen the ends and press them on to the pastry border. Cut six small shapes out of the remaining pastry, dampen them and press one on the end of each strip. Bake the tart in a fairly hot oven, 200°C/400°F/Gas 6, for 30 – 35 minutes until the pastry is set and golden-brown. Serve hot or cold with cream or custard.

BREAD AND BUTTER PUDDING

Serves 4

4 thin slices bread, crusts removed

25 g/1 oz butter

50 g/2 oz sultanas *or* currants

a pinch of grated nutmeg *or* cinnamon

450 ml/³/₄ pint milk

2 eggs

25 g/1 oz granulated sugar

Spread the bread slices with the butter. Cut the bread into squares or triangles and arrange in a greased 1.2 litre/2 pint pie dish in alternate layers, buttered side up, with the sultanas or currants. Sprinkle each layer lightly with spices. Arrange the top layer of bread in an attractive pattern. Warm the milk to approximately 65°C/149°F; do not let it come near the boil. Beat together the eggs and most of the sugar with a fork, and stir in the warmed milk. Strain the custard over the bread, sprinkle some nutmeg and the remaining sugar on top, and leave to stand for 30 minutes. Bake in a moderate oven, 180°C/350°F/Gas 4, for 30 – 40 minutes until set and lightly browned.

Bread and Butter Pudding

APPLE CHARLOTTE

Amos and Henry both enjoy this

Serves 5 – 6

450 g/1 lb cooking apples, peeled, cored and sliced
grated rind and juice of 1 lemon
100 g/4 oz soft light brown sugar
a pinch of ground cinnamon
8 – 10 large slices white bread, 5 mm/¼ inch thick, crusts removed
50 – 75 g/2 – 3 oz butter, melted
1 x 15 ml spoon/1 tablespoon caster sugar

Simmer the apples, lemon rind and juice with the sugar and cinnamon until the apples soften to a thick purée. Leave to cool.
Dip one slice of bread in the butter. Cut it into a round to fit the bottom of a well greased 15 cm/ 6 inch cake tin. Fill in any gaps with small pieces of bread. Dip the remaining bread slices in the butter.
Line the inside of the mould with six slices, touching one another. Fill the bread case with the cooled purée. Complete the case by fitting the top with more bread slices. Cover loosely with greased paper or foil, and bake in a moderate oven, 180°C/350°F/Gas 4, for 40 – 45 minutes. For serving, turn out and dredge with caster sugar.
Serve with bramble jelly and cream.

MY SPECIAL RICE PUDDING

Enjoyed greatly by both Amos and Henry

Serves 6

100 g/4 oz long-grain rice
1.2 litres/2 pints milk
2 – 3 eggs, separated
a pinch of salt
50 – 75 g/2 – 3 oz caster sugar
ground cinnamon

Wash the rice in cold water and put it into the top of a double boiler with the milk. Cook slowly for about 1 hour or until tender. Remove from the heat and leave to cool slightly. Stir the egg yolks, salt, sugar and cinnamon into the rice. Whisk the egg whites to the same consistency as the pudding and fold into the mixture. Pour into a buttered 2.1 litre/3½ pint pie dish and bake in a warm oven, 160°C/325°F/Gas 3, for 40 – 45 minutes until the top is brown.

Desserts

SUMMER PUDDING

Serves 6 – 8

900 g/2 lb soft red fruit, eg black and red currants, blackberries, raspberries and bilberries
100 – 175 g/4 – 6 oz caster sugar
a strip of lemon rind
8 – 10 slices day-old white bread (5 mm/¼ inch thick), crusts removed

Put the fruit into a bowl with sugar to taste and the lemon rind, and leave overnight.
Turn the fruit and sugar into a pan, discarding the lemon rind, and simmer for 2 – 3 minutes until very lightly cooked. Remove from the heat.
Cut a circle from one slice of bread to fit the bottom of a 1.5 litre/2½ pint pudding basin. Line the base and sides of the basin with bread, leaving no spaces. Fill in any gaps with small pieces of bread. Fill with the fruit and any juice it has made while cooking. Cover with bread slices. Place a flat plate and a 900 g/2 lb weight on top, and leave overnight, or longer if refrigerated.
Serve turned out, with chilled whipped cream.

APPLE SNOW

All the family enjoy this on a hot summer's day

Serves 6

4 large baking apples
juice and pared rind of 1 lemon
175 g/6 oz caster sugar
300 ml/½ pint milk
2 – 3 eggs, separated
1 x 5 ml spoon/1 teaspoon cornflour *or* arrowroot
4 individual sponge cakes

DECORATION

glacé cherries

Bake and purée the apples, then add the lemon juice to the purée, sweeten with 100 g/4 oz of the sugar and leave to cool.

Put the lemon rind into a small pan with the milk and heat gently for 15 minutes, then strain. Blend together the yolks and remaining sugar with the cornflour or arrowroot. Add the lemon-infused milk. Cook, stirring all the time, in a saucepan for 20 – 30 minutes or until the custard coats the back of the spoon. Leave to cool.

Split the sponge cakes in half and arrange them in the bottom of a glass dish. Pour the custard over them. Whisk the whites until they form stiff peaks, then fold into the apple purée. Pile this on top of the custard and decorate with the glacé cherries.

MY JUNKET

A recipe handed down to me by my mother

Serves 4

600 ml/1 pint milk
1 x 15 ml spoon/1 tablespoon sugar
a few drops vanilla essence
1 x 5 ml spoon/1 teaspoon rennet essence
grated nutmeg *or* ground cinnamon

Warm the milk to blood-heat (37°C/98.6°F approx) with the sugar and vanilla essence. Stir in the rennet essence and pour into four small dishes. Cover and leave to stand in a warm place for about 1 hour or until set. Do not move the dishes. Sprinkle with nutmeg or cinnamon and serve cold but not chilled.

PAT'S LEMON MERINGUE PIE

Serves 6

350 g/12 oz prepared shortcrust pastry (see page 49)
275 g/10 oz granulated sugar
3 x 15 ml spoons/3 tablespoons cornflour
3 x 15 ml spoons/3 tablespoons plain flour
a pinch of salt
300 ml/½ pint water
2 x 15 ml spoons/2 tablespoons butter
1 x 5 ml spoon/1 teaspoon grated lemon rind
75 ml/3 fl oz lemon juice
3 eggs, separated
75 g/3 oz caster sugar

Roll out the pastry on a lightly floured surface and use it to line a 22.5 cm/9 inch pie plate. Bake blind until golden-brown, then cool.

Meanwhile, mix the granulated sugar, cornflour, plain flour and salt in the top of a double boiler. Boil the water separately, and add it slowly to the dry mixture, stirring all the time. Bring the mixture to the boil, stirring all the time, then place the top of the double boiler over hot water, cover, and cook gently for 20 minutes. Draw the pan off the heat. Add the butter, lemon rind and lemon juice. Beat the yolks until just liquid, and add a little of the cooked mixture. Mix into the cooked ingredients. Replace over heat and cook, stirring all the time, until the mixture thickens. Remove from the heat and leave to cool.

Whisk the egg whites until stiff and fold in the caster sugar. Pour the lemon custard into the baked pastry case and top with the meringue, making sure that it covers the top completely. Bake in a moderate oven, 180°C/350°F/Gas 4, for 12 – 15 minutes, until the meringue is lightly browned. Cool before cutting.

Raspberry Fool

AMOS'S WALNUT TRIFLE

Serves 3 – 4

| 100 g/4 oz walnuts |
| 175 g/6 oz stale plain cake |
| 450 ml/³/₄ pint cold thick custard |
| 2 bananas, sliced |
| 2 x 15 ml spoons/2 tablespoons raspberry jam |

DECORATION

| angelica |
| glacé cherries |

RASPBERRY FOOL

Dolly enjoys this very much

Serves 6

| 675 g/1¹/₂ lb raspberries |
| sugar |
| 600 ml/1 pint double cream |

DECORATION

fresh raspberries *or* whipped cream

Rub the raspberries through a sieve, then sweeten to taste, and leave to cool. Whip the cream until it holds its shape, then fold into the fruit purée. Turn into a serving bowl and chill before serving. Decorate with fresh raspberries or whipped cream.

Reserve a few whole walnuts for decoration and chop the rest. Crumble the cake to give coarse crumbs, then mix together with enough custard to make a firm paste. Add the bananas, chopped nuts and the jam. Place in a serving dish and cover with the remaining custard. Cover with damp greaseproof paper to prevent a skin forming, and chill for about 1 hour. Decorate with the whole walnuts, angelica and cherries.

Our Weekly Baking Day

MUFFINS

All my visitors seem to enjoy these

450 g/1 lb strong white flour
1 x 5 ml spoon/1 teaspoon salt
25 g/1 oz butter *or* margarine
275 ml/9 fl oz milk
15 g/¹/₂ oz fresh yeast *or* 1 x 10 ml spoon/ 1 dessertspoon dried yeast
1 egg
fat for shallow frying

Sift together the flour and salt into a large bowl. Rub in the fat. Warm the milk until hand-hot. Blend the fresh yeast into the milk or reconstitute the dried yeast. Beat the egg into the yeast liquid. Stir the liquid into the flour to make a very soft dough. Beat the dough with your hand or a wooden spoon for about 5 minutes or until smooth and shiny. Put the bowl in a large, lightly oiled polythene bag and leave in a warm place for 1 – 2 hours, or until the dough has almost doubled in size. Beat again lightly.

Roll out the dough on a well floured surface to 1.25 cm/¹/₂ inch thickness. Using a plain 7.5 cm/ 3 inch cutter, cut into rounds. Place the rounds on a floured tray, cover with polythene, and leave to rise at room temperature for about 45 minutes or until puffy.

Lightly grease a griddle or heavy frying pan and heat until a bread cube browns in ¹/₄ minute. Cook the muffins on both sides for about 8 minutes until golden-brown.

To serve, split open each muffin around the edges almost to the centre. Toast slowly on both outer sides so that the heat penetrates to the centre of the muffin. Pull apart, butter thickly, put together again, and serve hot.

EMMERDALE FARMHOUSE BREAD

900 g/2 lb strong white flour
1 x 10 ml spoon/1 dessertspoon salt
1 x 10 ml spoon/1 dessertspoon sugar
25 g/1 oz lard
25 g/1 oz fresh yeast *or* 1 x 15 ml spoon/ 1 tablespoon dried yeast
600 ml/1 pint warm water
beaten egg *or* milk

Sift together the flour, salt and sugar into a large bowl. Rub in the lard. Blend the fresh yeast into the warm water or reconstitute the dried yeast. Add the yeast liquid to the flour mixture and mix to a soft dough. Turn on to a floured surface and knead for about 8 minutes or until the dough is smooth, elastic and no longer sticky. Place the dough in a large, lightly oiled polythene bag and leave in a warm place for about 1 hour or until the dough has doubled in size.

Knead the dough again until firm. Cut into two equal portions and form each into a loaf shape. Put into two greased 900 g/2 lb loaf tins and brush the surface with beaten egg or milk. Place the tins in the polythene bag and leave in a warm place for about 45 minutes or until the dough has doubled in size. Remove from the bag and bake in a very hot oven, 230°C/450°F/Gas 8, for 35 – 40 minutes until the loaves are crisp and golden-brown and sound hollow when tapped on the bottom.

Bara Brith

BARA BRITH

300 ml/½ pint milk

1 x 5 ml spoon/1 teaspoon sugar

25 g/1 oz fresh yeast

75 g/3 oz lard *or* butter

450 g/1 lb strong plain flour

50 g/2 oz cut mixed peel

175 g/6 oz seedless raisins

50 g/2 oz currants

75 g/3 oz soft brown sugar

1 x 5 ml spoon/1 teaspoon mixed spice

a pinch of salt

1 egg, beaten

honey for glazing

Warm the milk to tepid with the sugar. Blend the fresh yeast into the milk, and put to one side for 10 – 20 minutes until frothy. Rub the lard or butter into the flour. Stir in the peel, raisins, currants, brown sugar, mixed spice and salt. Make a well in the centre of the dry ingredients and add the yeast mixture and the beaten egg. Mix to a soft dough, place in a large, lightly oiled polythene bag, and leave in a warm place for about 2 hours until the dough has doubled in size.

Turn the dough out on to a floured surface and knead well. Put it into a greased 900 g/2 lb loaf tin, pressing it well into the corners. Return to the polythene bag, and leave to rise for a further 30 minutes. Remove from the bag and bake in a fairly hot oven, 200°C/400°F/Gas 6, for 15 minutes. Reduce the heat to warm, 160°C/325°F/Gas 3, and bake for about 1¼ hours.

Turn the bread out on to a wire rack, and brush the top with clear warm honey while still warm. Serve sliced, spread with butter.

Chelsea Buns

CHELSEA BUNS

450 g/1 lb strong white flour
1 x 5 ml spoon/1 teaspoon sugar
250 ml/8 fl oz milk
25 g/1 oz fresh yeast *or* 1 x 15 ml spoon/ 1 tablespoon dried yeast
1 x 5 ml spoon/1 teaspoon salt
50 g/2 oz butter
1 egg
1 x 15 ml spoon/1 tablespoon butter
175 g/6 oz currants
50 g/2 oz chopped mixed peel
100 g/4 oz soft brown sugar
honey for glazing

GLAZE

100 g/4 oz caster sugar
4 x 15 ml spoons/4 tablespoons water

Sift about 75 g/3 oz of the flour and the sugar into a large bowl. Warm the milk until hand-hot and blend in the fresh yeast or sprinkle on the dried yeast. Pour the yeast liquid into the flour and sugar and beat well. Leave the bowl in a warm place for 20 minutes. Sift the remaining flour and the salt into a bowl. Rub in the butter. Beat the egg into the frothy yeast mixture and add the flour and fat. Mix to a soft dough.

Turn the dough on to a lightly floured surface and knead for about 6 minutes or until smooth and no longer sticky. Place in a large, lightly oiled polythene bag and leave in a warm place for about 1 hour or until doubled in size. On a floured surface, roll the dough into a 50 cm/20 inch square. Melt the 1 x 15 ml spoon/ 1 tablespoon butter and brush it all over the surface of the dough. Sprinkle with the dried fruit and sugar. Roll up the dough like a Swiss roll, then cut the roll into 16 equal pieces. Place the buns, about 2.5 cm/1 inch apart, on a greased baking sheet with the cut side uppermost. Place the baking sheet in the polythene bag and leave in a warm place for about 30 minutes or until the buns have joined together and are light and puffy. Bake in a hot oven, 220°C/425°F/Gas 7, for 20 – 25 minutes until golden-brown.

Meanwhile, prepare the glaze. Dissolve the sugar in the water for 2 minutes, then brush over the warm buns, and cool on a wire rack.

SANDIE'S CRUMPETS

225 g/8 oz strong white flour
1 x 2.5 ml spoon/½ teaspoon salt
1 x 2.5 ml spoon/½ teaspoon sugar
100 ml/4 fl oz milk
150 ml/¼ pint water
15 g/½ oz fresh yeast *or* 1 x 10 ml spoon/ 1 dessertspoon dried yeast
a pinch of bicarbonate of soda
1 x 15 ml spoon/1 tablespoon warm water
fat for shallow frying

Sift together the flour, salt and sugar into a large bowl. Warm the milk and water until hand-hot. Blend the fresh yeast into the liquid or reconstitute the dried yeast. Add the yeast liquid to the flour and beat to a smooth batter. Cover with a large, lightly oiled polythene bag and leave in a warm place for about 45 minutes or until the dough has doubled in size. Dissolve the bicarbonate of soda in the 15 ml spoon/1 tablespoon warm water and beat into the batter mixture. Cover and leave to rise again for 20 minutes.

Grease a griddle or thick frying pan and heat until a bread cube browns in ¼ minute. Grease metal rings, poaching rings or large plain biscuit cutters, about 7.5 cm/3 inches in diameter. Place the rings on the hot griddle. Pour about 1 x 15 ml spoonful/1 tablespoon of batter into each ring so that the batter is about 2.5 mm/⅛ inch deep. Cook until the top is set and the bubbles have burst. Remove the ring and turn the crumpet over. Cook the other side for 2 – 3 minutes only until firm but barely coloured. Crumpets should be pale on top. Repeat until all the batter has been used up. Serve toasted, hot, with butter.

MY GRANDMOTHER'S LARDY CAKE

400 g/14 oz risen Farmhouse Bread dough (see page 72)
125 g/5 oz lard
100 g/4 oz caster sugar
100 g/4 oz sultanas *or* currants
1 x 5 ml spoon/1 teaspoon mixed spice

GLAZE

1 x 10 ml spoon/1 dessertspoon caster sugar
1 x 15 ml spoon/1 tablespoon water

On a floured surface, roll out the dough to a strip 2.5 cm/1 inch thick. Place one-third of the lard in small pats over the surface of the dough. Sprinkle one-third of the sugar, dried fruit and spice over it. Fold the dough into three. Repeat the rolling and folding twice more, using the remaining ingredients. Roll out to fit a 20 cm/8 inch square slab cake or baking tin. Score diamond shapes in the surface of the dough with a sharp knife. Place the tin in a large, lightly oiled polythene bag and leave in a warm place for about 45 minutes or until the dough has risen by half. Bake in a fairly hot oven, 200°C/400°F/Gas 6, for 40 minutes until crisp and golden-brown.

To make the glaze, boil together the sugar and water until syrupy, and brush over the surface of the warm cake.

Sandie bakes some truly delicious cakes, pastry and breads

MADEIRA CAKE

175 g/6 oz butter *or* margarine

175 g/6 oz caster sugar

4 eggs, beaten

225 g/8 oz plain flour

2 x 5 ml spoons/2 teaspoons baking powder

a pinch of salt

grated rind of 1 lemon

caster sugar for dredging

2 thin slices candied *or* glacé citron peel

Cream together the fat and sugar until light and
fluffy. Add the eggs gradually to the creamed
mixture, beating well after each addition. Sift
together the flour, baking powder and salt, and fold
into the creamed mixture. Mix in the lemon rind.
Mix well. Turn into a greased and lined 15 cm/
6 inch cake tin and dredge the top with caster
sugar. Bake in a moderate oven, 180°C/350°F/Gas
4, for 20 minutes, then lay the slices of peel on top.
Bake for a further 45 – 50 minutes.

Date and Walnut Loaf

Pineapple Upside-down Cake

PINEAPPLE UPSIDE-DOWN CAKE

225 g/8 oz canned pineapple rings

100 g/4 oz butter

275 g/10 oz soft dark brown sugar

8 maraschino *or* glacé cherries

450 g/1 lb self-raising flour

1 x 5 ml spoon/1 teaspoon ground cinnamon

1 x 5 ml spoon/1 teaspoon grated nutmeg

2 eggs

300 ml/½ pint milk

Drain the pineapple rings, reserving the syrup.
Melt 50 g/2 oz of the butter in a 20 cm/8 inch
square baking tin. Add 100 g/4 oz of the sugar and
1 x 15 ml spoon/1 tablespoon of pineapple syrup;
mix well. Arrange the pineapple rings in an even
pattern in the bottom of the tin, and place a cherry
in the centre of each ring.
Sift together the flour, cinnamon and nutmeg.
Beat the eggs with the remaining brown sugar.
Melt the remaining butter and add to the eggs and
sugar with the milk; mix into the spiced flour. Pour
this mixture carefully over the fruit in the baking
tin without disturbing it. Bake in a moderate oven,
180°C/350°F/Gas 4, for 45 – 50 minutes. Remove
the tin from the oven and at once turn upside-down
on to a plate; allow the caramel to run over the
cake before removing the baking tin.
Serve warm with cream as a dessert, or cold for
afternoon tea.

DATE AND WALNUT LOAF

Jackie likes to take a slice (or several slices!) when he's off to the fields

250 g/9 oz plain flour
50 g/2 oz cornflour
175 g/6 oz caster sugar
1 x 5 ml spoon/1 teaspoon salt
50 g/2 oz walnuts, chopped
200 g/7 oz cooking dates, chopped
2 x 15 ml spoons/2 tablespoons oil
1 size 1 – 2 egg
2 x 5 ml spoons/2 teaspoons bicarbonate of soda
300 ml/¹/₂ pint boiling water

Sift the flour, cornflour, sugar and salt into a bowl, then add the walnuts and dates. Whisk together the oil and egg and add to the flour, fruit and nuts. Dissolve the bicarbonate of soda in the boiling water, and stir into the other ingredients. Beat well to a soft consistency. Pour into a greased 900 g/2 lb loaf tin and bake in a moderate oven, 180°C/350°F/Gas 4, for about 1 hour until firm to the touch. Leave to cool slightly before turning out of the tin. Serve sliced, spread with butter.

SANDIE'S FRUIT LOAF

350 g/12 oz mixed dried fruit
175 g/6 oz dark Barbados sugar
250 ml/8 fl oz strong hot tea
1 egg, beaten
350 g/12 oz self-raising flour

Put the fruit and sugar in a large bowl. Pour the hot tea over them, cover and leave overnight. Next day, stir the egg into the tea mixture. Stir in the flour and mix well. Put the mixture into a lined and greased 900 g/2 lb loaf tin and bake in a moderate oven, 180°/350°F/Gas 4, for 1¹/₂ hours. Cool on a wire rack. When cold, wrap in foil and store in a tin.

GINGERBREAD

First made by my mother and enjoyed ever since

225 g/8 oz plain flour
¹/₂ x 2.5 ml spoon/¹/₄ teaspoon salt
2 – 3 x 5 ml spoons/2 – 3 teaspoons ground ginger
1 x 2.5 ml spoon/¹/₂ teaspoon bicarbonate of soda
50 – 100 g/2 – 4 oz lard
50 g/2 oz brown sugar
100 g/4 oz golden syrup or black treacle (or a mixture)
milk
1 egg, beaten

Sift together the flour, salt, ginger and bicarbonate of soda into a bowl. Warm the fat, sugar and syrup in a saucepan until the fat has melted. Do not allow the mixture to become hot. Add enough milk to the egg to make up to 150 ml/¹/₄ pint. Add the melted mixture to the dry ingredients with the beaten egg and milk. Stir thoroughly; the mixture should run easily off the spoon. Pour into a greased and lined 15 cm/6 inch square tin and bake in a warm oven, 160°C/325°F/Gas 3, for 1¹/₄ – 1¹/₂ hours until firm to the touch.

Gingerbread

MY SEED CAKE

225 g/8 oz plain flour

½ x 2.5 ml spoon/¼ teaspoon salt

1 x 2.5 ml spoon/¼ teaspoon baking powder

4 eggs

175 g/6 oz butter *or* margarine

175 g/6 oz caster sugar

3 x 5 ml spoons/3 teaspoons caraway seeds

1 x 15 ml spoon/1 tablespoon milk

Sift together the flour, salt and baking powder. Beat the eggs in a basin and stand it in tepid water (or make sure you use eggs at room temperature). Beat the fat until very soft, add the sugar, and cream well together until light and fluffy. Add the eggs gradually, beating well after each addition. If the mixture shows signs of curdling, add a little flour. Fold in the dry ingredients and caraway seeds lightly but thoroughly. Add the milk if too stiff. Put into a lined and greased 15 cm/6 inch round cake tin, smooth the top and make a hollow in the centre. Bake in a moderate oven, 180°C/350°F/Gas 4, for 30 minutes, then reduce the heat to warm, 160°C/325°F/Gas 3, and bake for a further 50 minutes or until firm to the touch.

DUNDEE CAKE

225 g/8 oz plain flour

1 x 2.5 ml spoon/½ teaspoon baking powder

½ x 2.5 ml spoon/¼ teaspoon salt

175 g/6 oz butter

175 g/6 oz caster sugar

4 eggs

100 g/4 oz glacé cherries, cut into quarters

175 g/6 oz currants

175 g/6 oz sultanas

100 g/4 oz seedless raisins

50 g/2 oz mixed peel

50 g/2 oz ground almonds

grated rind of 1 lemon

50 g/2 oz blanched split almonds

Sift together the flour, baking powder and salt. Cream the butter and sugar together well, and beat in the eggs. Fold the flour, cherries, dried fruit, peel and ground almonds into the creamed mixture. Add the lemon rind and mix well. Put into a greased and lined 17.5 cm/7 inch cake tin and make a slight hollow in the centre. Bake in a moderate oven, 180°C/350°F/Gas 4, for 20 minutes, when the hollow should have filled in. Arrange the split almonds on top. Return the cake to the oven, bake for a further 40 – 50 minutes, then reduce the heat to warm, 160°C/325°F/Gas 3, and bake for another hour.

Sandie's Sandwich Cake

SANDIE'S SANDWICH CAKE

175 g/6 oz butter *or* margarine
175 g/6 oz caster sugar
3 eggs, beaten
175 g/6 oz self-raising flour
a pinch of salt
double cream
raspberry *or* other jam
extra caster sugar

Cream together the fat and sugar until light and fluffy. Add the eggs gradually, beating well after each addition. Sift together the flour and salt, then stir into the mixture, lightly but thoroughly, until evenly mixed. Divide between two greased and lined 17.5 cm/7 inch sandwich tins and bake in a moderate oven, 180°C/350°F/Gas 4 for 25 – 30 minutes. When cold, whip the cream until stiff, then sandwich the cake with the cream and jam, and sprinkle the top with caster sugar.

SANDIE'S SWISS ROLL

3 eggs
75 g/3 oz caster sugar
1 x 2.5 ml spoon/¹/₂ teaspoon baking powder
75 g/3 oz plain flour
a pinch of salt
jam
caster sugar for dredging

Whisk the eggs and sugar together in a bowl over a pan of hot water, taking care that the base does not touch the water. Whisk for 10 – 15 minutes until thick and creamy. Remove from the pan and whisk until cold. Sift the baking powder with the flour and salt, and fold in lightly. Pour into a greased and lined 20 x 30 cm/8 x 12 inch Swiss roll tin and bake in a preheated hot oven, 220°C/425°F/Gas 7, for 10 minutes. Meanwhile, warm the jam, if used.

When the cake is cooked, turn it on to a large sheet of greaseproof paper dusted with caster sugar. Peel off the lining paper. Trim off any crisp edges. Spread the cake with the warmed jam and roll up tightly. Dredge with caster sugar and place on a cooling rack with the cut edge underneath.

Maids of Honour and *Pat's Cream Horns*

MAIDS OF HONOUR

Makes 20

450 g/1 lb prepared puff pastry (see page 44)

225 g/8 oz ground almonds

100 g/4 oz caster sugar

2 eggs

25 g/1 oz flour

4 x 15 ml spoons/4 tablespoons single cream

2 x 15 ml spoons/2 tablespoons orange flower water

Roll out the pastry on a lightly floured surface and use it to line twenty 7.5 cm/3 inch patty tins. Mix together the ground almonds and sugar. Add the eggs, and mix in the flour, cream and orange flower water. Put the mixture into the pastry cases and bake in a fairly hot oven, 200°C/400°F/Gas 6, for about 15 minutes or until the filling is firm and golden-brown.

PAT'S CREAM HORNS

225 g/8 oz prepared puff pastry (see page 44)

beaten egg and milk for glazing

3 x 15 ml spoons/3 tablespoons sieved raspberry jam

4 x 15 ml spoons/4 tablespoons liqueur-flavoured whipped cream

2 x 15 ml spoons/2 tablespoons finely chopped nuts

Roll out the pastry 5 mm/¼ inch thick on a lightly floured surface and cut into strips 35 cm/14 inches long and 2.5 cm/1 inch wide. Moisten the strips with cold water. Wind each strip round a cornet mould, working from the point upward, keeping the moistened surface on the outside. Lay the horns on a dampened baking tray, with the final overlap of the pastry strip underneath. Leave in a cool place for 1 hour.
Brush the horns with beaten egg and milk, and bake in a preheated hot oven, 220°C/425°F/Gas 7, for 10 – 15 minutes or until golden-brown. Remove the moulds and return the horns to the oven for 5 minutes. Cool completely on a wire rack. When cold, put a very little jam in the bottom of each horn. Fill the horns with the cream, and sprinkle with the chopped nuts.

SANDIE'S JAM TURNOVERS

300 g/11 oz prepared shortcrust pastry
(see page 49)

2 x 15 ml spoons/2 tablespoons jam

1 x 15 ml spoon/1 tablespoon caster sugar

Roll out the pastry 2.5 mm/⅛ inch thick on a lightly floured surface and cut into rounds using a 10 cm/4 inch cutter. Place spoonfuls of jam in the centre of each pastry round. Moisten the edges with water and fold the pastry over the filling. Press the edges well together and crimp or decorate with a fork. Place the turnovers on a baking sheet, brush with water, and dredge with the caster sugar. Bake in a fairly hot oven, 200°C/400°F/ Gas 6, for about 20 minutes or until golden-brown.

ECCLES CAKES

Makes 12 – 14

450 g/1 lb prepared flaky or rough puff pastry
(see page 38)

25 g/1 oz butter or margarine

1 x 15 ml spoon/1 tablespoon sugar

75 g/3 oz currants

25 g/1 oz cut mixed peel

½ x 2.5 ml spoon/¼ teaspoon mixed spice

½ x 2.5 ml spoon/¼ teaspoon grated nutmeg

caster sugar

Roll out the pastry 5 mm/¼ inch thick on a lightly floured surface and cut into 12 – 14 rounds using a 10 cm/4 inch pastry cutter. Cream together the fat and sugar, add the currants, peel and spices, and place spoonfuls of the mixture in the centre of each pastry round. Gather the edges of each round together to form a ball. With the smooth side uppermost, form into a flat cake. Make two cuts in the top of each cake with a sharp knife. Brush with water and dust with caster sugar. Put on a baking sheet and bake in a preheated hot oven, 220°C/425°F/Gas 7, for 20 minutes or until golden-brown.

Eccles Cakes

Dolly's Raspberry Buns

DOLLY'S RASPBERRY BUNS

Makes 12 – 14

225 g/8 oz self-raising flour
¹/₂ x 2.5 ml spoon/¹/₄ teaspoon salt
75 g/3 oz margarine
75 g/3 oz sugar
milk
1 egg, beaten
4 – 5 x 15 ml spoons/4 – 5 tablespoons raspberry jam
egg *or* milk
caster sugar

Sift or mix together the flour and salt. Cut the margarine into small pieces in the flour, and rub in until the mixture resembles fine breadcrumbs. Stir in the sugar. Add enough milk to the egg to make up to 150 ml/¹/₄ pint. Add the liquid to the dry ingredients, and mix with a fork to a stiff consistency. This produces a sticky mixture which supports the fork. Divide into 12 – 14 balls and make a deep dent in the centre of each ball. Drop 1 x 5 ml spoon/1 teaspoon raspberry jam inside each, then close the mixture over the jam. Brush with egg or milk and sprinkle with sugar. Place on a well-greased baking sheet, spaced well apart, and bake in a fairly hot oven, 200°C/400°F/Gas 6, for 15 – 20 minutes until firm to the touch on the underside.

TREACLE SCONES

As enjoyed by all the Family

225 g/8 oz plain flour
¹/₂ x 2.5 ml spoon/¹/₄ teaspoon salt
1 x 2.5 ml spoon/¹/₂ teaspoon ground cinnamon
1 x 2.5 ml spoon/¹/₂ teaspoon mixed spice
50 g/2 oz butter *or* margarine
1 x 5 ml spoon/1 teaspoon bicarbonate of soda
1 x 10 ml spoon/1 dessertspoon cream of tartar
2 x 10 ml spoons/2 dessertspoons light soft brown sugar
150 ml/¹/₄ pint milk
1 x 15 ml spoon/1 tablespoon warmed black treacle
milk *or* beaten egg for glazing

Sift together the flour, salt and spices into a large bowl. Rub in the fat, sift in the dry raising agents, add the sugar and mix well. Add the milk and treacle, and mix lightly to form a soft spongy dough. Knead very lightly until smooth.
Roll out the dough on a floured surface to 1.25 – 2.5 cm/¹/₂ – 1 inch thickness and cut into rounds, using a 5 cm/2 inch cutter. Re-roll the trimmings, and re-cut. Place the scones on a greased baking sheet and brush the tops with milk or beaten egg. Bake in a hot oven, 220°C/425°F/Gas 7, for 7 – 10 minutes until well risen and golden-brown. Cool on a wire rack.

LEMON TARTLETS

Pat makes these specially for Jackie and Sandie

Makes 12

200 g/7 oz prepared shortcrust pastry (see page 49)
50 g/2 oz butter
50 g/2 oz sugar
1 egg
grated rind and juice of ¹/₂ lemon
2 x 5 ml spoons/2 teaspoons icing sugar

Roll out the pastry on a lightly floured surface and use it to line twelve 7.5 cm/3 inch patty tins. Cream together the butter and sugar until pale and fluffy, then beat in the egg. Add the lemon rind and juice. Fill the pastry cases with the mixture and bake in a fairly hot oven, 200°C/400°F/Gas 6, for 15 – 20 minutes or until set. Leave to cool. Sift the icing sugar over the tartlets.

Dropped Scones

DROPPED SCONES

Pat likes these thickly spread with butter, jam and cream

225 g/8 oz plain flour
1 x 5 ml spoon/1 teaspoon salt
25 g/1 oz caster sugar
1 x 10 ml spoon/1 dessertspoon cream of tartar
1 x 5 ml spoon/1 teaspoon bicarbonate of soda
1 egg
150 ml/¼ pint milk (approx)

Sift together the dry ingredients three times. Add the egg and milk gradually and mix to a smooth thick batter. Heat a lightly greased griddle or a very thick frying pan. Drop dessertspoonfuls of the mixture on to the griddle or pan. Tiny bubbles will appear and when these burst, turn the scones over, using a palette knife. Cook the underside until golden-brown, then cool the scones in a clean tea-towel on a rack. The scones will take about 3 minutes to cook on the first side and about 2 minutes after turning.

DOLLY'S CHERRY TARTLETS

Makes 12

200 g/7 oz prepared shortcrust pastry (see page 49)
375 g/13 oz canned cherries in syrup
25 g/1 oz lump sugar
1 x 5 ml spoon/1 teaspoon arrowroot
1 x 10 ml spoon/1 dessertspoon lemon juice
150 ml/¼ pint double cream

Roll out the pastry on a lightly floured surface and use to line twelve 7.5 cm/3 inch patty tins or small boat-shaped moulds. Bake blind, then cool.
    Drain and stone the cherries, reserving the syrup. Place a layer of cherries in the pastry cases. Make up the syrup to 150 ml/¼ pint with water. Heat the liquid and dissolve the sugar in it, bring to the boil, and boil for 5 minutes. Blend the arrowroot to a smooth paste with the lemon juice and add to the syrup, stirring all the time. Boil for 2 minutes until the syrup is clear and thick. Cool slightly, then pour a little of the glaze over the cherries. Leave to set. Whip the cream until stiff, and pipe a rosette on each tartlet.

My Cream Slices

MY CREAM SLICES

All the men are partial to these

Makes 8

225 g/8 oz prepared puff pastry (see page 44)
100 g/4 oz prepared royal icing
2 × 15 ml spoons/2 tablespoons smooth seedless jam
150 ml/¼ pint sweetened whipped cream
100 g/4 oz prepared white glacé icing (see page 85)

Roll out the pastry 1.25 cm/½ inch thick on a lightly floured surface into a neat rectangle. Cut it into eight oblong pieces 10 × 2.5 cm/4 × 1 inch. Place on a baking sheet and spread the tops thinly with royal icing. Bake in a preheated hot oven, 220°C/425°F/Gas 7, for 20 minutes or until the pastry is well risen and the icing is slightly browned. Leave to cool completely.
When cold, split the pastry in half crossways. Spread the top of the bottom half with jam, and the bottom of the top half with cream, then sandwich the halves together again. Spread glacé icing on top of each slice, over the browned royal icing.

ROYAL ICING

For the top and sides of a 20 cm/8 inch cake
Makes 450 g/1 lb (approx)

2 egg whites
1 × 5 ml spoon/1 teaspoon lemon juice
450 g/1 lb icing sugar, sifted
1 × 5 ml spoon/1 teaspoon glycerine

Put the egg whites and lemon juice into a bowl and, using a wooden spoon, beat just enough to liquefy the whites slightly. Add half the sugar, a little at a time, and beat for 10 minutes. Add the rest of the sugar gradually, and beat for another 10 minutes until the icing is white and forms peaks when the spoon is drawn up from the mixture. Add the glycerine while mixing. Use as required.

GLACÉ ICING

Makes 100 g/4 oz (approx)

2 x 10 ml spoons/2 dessertspoons water (approx)
100 g/4 oz icing sugar, sifted

Put 1 x 15 ml spoon/1 tablespoon water into a small non-stick or enamel saucepan with the icing sugar. Warm very gently, without making the pan too hot to touch on the underside. Beat well with a wooden spoon. The icing should coat the back of the spoon thickly. If it is too thick, add the extra water; if too thin add a very little extra sifted icing sugar. Use at once.

SANDIE'S FLAPJACKS

50 g/2 oz margarine
50 g/2 oz soft light brown sugar
2 x 15 ml spoons/2 tablespoons golden syrup
100 g/4 oz rolled oats

Melt the margarine, add the sugar and syrup, and warm gently. Do not boil. Remove from the heat and stir in the oats. Press into a greased 27.5 x 17.5 cm/11 x 7 inch tin. Bake in a warm oven, 160°C/325°F/Gas 3, for 25 minutes or until firm. Cut into fingers while still warm and leave in the tin to cool.

SHREWSBURY BISCUITS

100 g/4 oz butter *or* margarine
100 g/4 oz caster sugar
1 egg yolk *or* ½ beaten egg
1 x 5 ml spoon/1 teaspoon grated lemon rind
225 g/8 oz self-raising flour

Cream the fat and sugar until light and fluffy, then beat in the egg and lemon rind. Fold in the flour, using a knife and then the fingers. On a lightly floured surface, knead lightly and roll out to 5 mm – 1.25 cm/¼ – ½ inch thick. Cut into rounds with a 5 cm/2 inch cutter. Re-roll and re-cut any trimmings. Prick the surface of the biscuits in two or three places with a fork. Place on a well-greased baking sheet, and bake in a warm oven, 160°C/325°F/Gas 3, for 30 – 40 minutes. Leave on the baking sheet for 5 minutes before transferring to a wire rack. Store in an airtight tin when cold.

Shrewsbury Biscuits and Sandie's Flapjacks

MY SPECIAL BISCUIT SELECTION — NUTTY COFFEE ROUNDS

100 g/4 oz plain flour
2 x 5 ml spoons/2 teaspoons instant coffee powder
100 g/4 oz butter
50 g/2 oz caster sugar
50 g/2 oz finely chopped walnuts

Sift together the flour and coffee. Cream the butter with the sugar until light and fluffy. Add the walnuts, then stir in the flour and coffee. Put teaspoons of the mixture on to a greased baking sheet, spaced well apart, and bake in a fairly hot oven, 190°C/375°F/Gas 5, for 15 – 20 minutes. Leave on the sheet for a few minutes before transferring to a wire rack. Store in an airtight tin when cold.

MY SPECIAL BISCUIT SELECTION — GINGER SNAPS

225 g/8 oz self-raising flour
a pinch of salt
1 x 5 ml spoon/1 teaspoon ground ginger
100 g/4 oz soft light brown sugar
75 g/3 oz margarine
100 g/4 oz golden syrup
1 egg, beaten

Sift together the flour, salt, ginger and sugar. Melt the margarine and syrup in a medium-sized saucepan. When the fat has melted, add the dry ingredients and egg alternately and beat until smooth and thick. Using two teaspoons, place rounds of mixture on to well-greased baking sheets, spaced well apart, and bake in a warm oven, 160°C/325°F/Gas 3, for 15 minutes. Leave on the sheets for a few moments before transferring to a wire rack. Store in an airtight tin when cold.

My special biscuit selection – Buttery Whirls, Nutty Coffee Rounds, Ginger Snaps and Shortbread

MY SPECIAL BISCUIT SELECTION — BUTTERY WHIRLS

175 g/6 oz butter
50 g/2 oz icing sugar, sifted
1 x 2.5 ml spoon/¹/₂ teaspoon vanilla essence
175 g/6 oz plain flour, sifted
glacé cherries, halved

Cream the butter with the sugar and vanilla essence until light and fluffy. Stir in the flour, then transfer the mixture to a forcing bag with a star-shaped nozzle. Pipe whirls on to buttered baking sheets, and put a cherry on to each one. Bake in a moderate oven, 160°C/325°F/Gas 3, for 20 minutes or until pale gold. Leave on the sheets for 5 minutes, then transfer to a wire rack. Store in an airtight tin when cold.

MY SPECIAL BISCUIT SELECTION — SHORTBREAD

100 g/4 oz plain flour
¹/₂ x 2.5 ml spoon/¹/₄ teaspoon salt
50 g/2 oz rice flour, ground rice or semolina
50 g/2 oz caster sugar
100 g/4 oz butter

Mix together all the dry ingredients. Rub in the butter until the mixture binds together to a paste. Shape into a large round about 1.25 cm/¹/₂ inch thick. Pinch up the edges to decorate. Place on an upturned greased baking sheet, and prick with a fork. Bake in a moderate oven, 180°C/350°F/Gas 4, for 40 – 45 minutes. Cut into eight wedges while still warm.

OATMEAL BISCUITS

First made by my mother and always enjoyed (between meals!) by Dad

100 g/4 oz medium oatmeal
100 g/4 oz self-raising flour
1 x 2.5 ml spoon/¹/₂ teaspoon salt
a pinch of sugar
100 g/4 oz butter or margarine
2 x 15 ml spoons/2 tablespoons beaten egg
2 x 15 ml spoons/2 tablespoons water

Mix all the dry ingredients together and rub in the fat. Mix the egg with the water and use this to bind the dry ingredients together into a stiff paste. Roll out on a lightly floured surface to just under 1.25 cm/¹/₂ inch thick. Cut into rounds with a 5 cm/2 inch cutter. Prick the surface of the biscuits with a fork and place on a greased baking sheet. Bake in a moderate oven, 180°C/350°F/Gas 4, for 15 – 20 minutes.

My Special Preserves

RASPBERRY JAM

Yield 2.25 kg/5 lb (approx)

1.1 kg/2½ lb raspberries

1.35 kg/3 lb sugar

Do not wash the raspberries unless absolutely necessary; if they have to be washed, drain very thoroughly. Bring the fruit gently to the boil without any added water, then boil rapidly for 5 minutes. Warm the sugar. Draw the pan off the heat, add the warmed sugar, then stir well over low heat until all the sugar has dissolved. Bring to the boil and boil rapidly for 1 minute. Remove from the heat, skim quickly, pot at once, cover and label. This jam does not set firmly, but it has a delicious fresh flavour.

Apricot Jam

STRAWBERRY JAM

Yield 2.25 kg/5 lb (approx)

1.35 kg/3 lb strawberries, hulled

juice of 1 lemon

1.35 kg/3 lb sugar

Put the strawberries and lemon juice in a preserving pan. Heat gently for 10 minutes, stirring all the time, to reduce the volume. Add the sugar, stir over low heat until dissolved, then bring to the boil and boil rapidly until setting point is reached. Remove from the heat and skim. Leave the jam undisturbed to cool for about 20 minutes until a skin forms on the surface and the fruit sinks. Stir gently to distribute the strawberries. Pot and cover with discs. Tie down and label when cold. This jam will have cooled too much for the use of a twist-top.

APRICOT JAM

Yield 2.25 kg/5 lb (approx)

1.35 kg/3 lb apricots

300 ml/½ pint water

1.35 kg/3 lb sugar

Wash, halve and stone the fruit and put it into a preserving pan with the water. If desired, crack a few of the stones, remove and halve the kernels and blanch them by dipping in boiling water. Add the halved kernels to the pan. Simmer until tender and reduced by one-third. Add the sugar, and stir over low heat until dissolved. Bring to the boil and boil rapidly until setting point is reached. Remove from the heat, skim, pot, cover and label.

FIVE FRUIT MARMALADE

Yield 2.25 kg/5 lb (approx)

900 g/2 lb fruit: 1 orange, 1 grapefruit, 1 lemon, 1 large apple, 1 pear

2.4 litres/4 pints water

1.35 kg/3 lb sugar

Peel the citrus fruit, and shred the peel finely. Scrape off the pith, and chop the flesh coarsely. Put the pips and pith in a basin with 600 ml/1 pint water. Put the peel and chopped flesh in another basin with the remaining water. Soak for 24 hours, if liked. Strain the pips and pith through a muslin bag and tie loosely. Put into a preserving pan with the fruit, peel and all the liquid. Peel and dice the apple and pear and add to the other fruit. Bring to the boil, reduce the heat and simmer for 1¼ hours until the volume is reduced by one-third. Remove the bag and squeeze out the juice. Add the sugar, and stir over low heat until dissolved. Bring to the boil and boil rapidly for about 30 minutes or until setting point is reached. Remove from the heat, skim, cool slightly, then stir, pot, cover and label.

COARSE-CUT MARMALADE

Yield 4.5 kg/10 lb (approx)

1.35 kg/3 lb Seville oranges, cut in half

2 lemons, cut in half

4.8 litres/8 pints water

2.7 kg/6 lb sugar

1 x 15 ml spoon/1 tablespoon black treacle

Squeeze out and strain the juice of the oranges and lemons. Tie the pips and pulp loosely in a muslin bag. Slice the peel into medium-thick shreds, and put into a preserving pan with the juice, muslin bag and water. Simmer for about 1½ – 2 hours, or until the peel is tender and the liquid reduced by at least one-third. Remove the bag of pips and squeeze the juice out gently. Remove the pan from the heat, add the sugar and treacle, then stir over low heat until the sugar is dissolved. Bring to the boil and boil rapidly until setting point is reached. Remove from the heat, skim, cool until a skin forms, then stir, pot, cover and label.

APPLE AND APRICOT CONSERVE

Yield 4.5 kg/10 lb (approx)

450 g/1 lb dried apricots, chopped

1.2 litres/2 pints cider

1.8 kg/4 lb Bramley cooking apples

4 x 10 ml spoons/4 dessertspoons lemon juice

2.7 kg/6 lb granulated sugar

Put the apricots in a large pan, cover with cider and leave overnight.
Next day, peel, core and chop the apples into chunks and put into a preserving pan. Add the apricots and cider. Bring to the boil and simmer gently until the fruit is soft. Add the lemon juice and sugar, and stir gently over heat until the sugar is thoroughly dissolved. Bring rapidly to the boil, stirring from time to time to prevent the mixture sticking to the base of the pan. Test the syrup on a plate for set, and when ready, put the conserve into warm, dry pots, cover at once and label.

BLACKBERRY AND APPLE JAM

Yield 2.25 kg/5 lb (approx)

350 g/12 oz sour apples, peeled, cored and sliced

300 ml/½ pint water

900 g/2 lb blackberries

1.35 kg/3 lb sugar

Cook the apples in half the water until pulped. Put the blackberries in another pan with the rest of the water and cook until tender. (If the two fruits are cooked together, the apple will not cook to a pulp.) Mix the cooked fruits in a preserving pan and add the sugar. Stir over low heat until the sugar is dissolved, then bring to the boil and boil rapidly until setting point is reached. Remove from the heat, skim, pot, cover and label.

A selection of my special preserves

APPLE JELLY

1.8 kg/4 lb well-flavoured crab-apples, cooking apples *or* windfalls, cut up but not cored

1.8 – 2.4 litres/3 – 4 pints water

25 g/1 oz ginger root *or* thinly pared rind of 1 lemon

sugar (see Method)

If windfall apples are used, weigh after removing the damaged parts Use just enough water to cover, bruise the ginger, if used, add the chosen flavouring and simmer for about 1 hour until tender and well mashed. If the apples do not break down, press them after 30 minutes with a potato masher. Test for pectin, and if the clot is satisfactory, strain the juice through a scalded jelly bag. Leave to drip for 1 hour, then measure the extract, return it to the cleaned pan, and heat gently. Weigh and add the required sugar (usually 900 g/2 lb for each 1.2 litres/2 pints of extract). Stir over low heat until dissolved. Bring the jelly to a steady boil and test for set after 10 minutes. Remove from the heat, skim carefully, pot, cover and label.

REDCURRANT JELLY

1.8 kg/4 lb large, juicy redcurrants *or* redcurrants and white currants mixed

sugar (see Method)

Put the fruit in a preserving pan, without any water, and heat very gently for about 45 minutes or until the currants are softened and well cooked. Mash, then strain the pulp through a scalded jelly bag. Leave it to drip for 1 hour. Measure the extract and return it to the cleaned pan. Add 900 g/2 lb sugar for each 1.2 litres/2 pints of extract. Bring to the boil, stirring all the time, then boil, without stirring, for 1 minute. Skim the jelly quickly, and immediately pour it into warmed jars before it has a chance to set in the pan. Cover and label.

MINT JELLY

900 g/2 lb green apples, cut into quarters

600 ml/1 pint water

a small bunch of fresh mint

600 ml/1 pint vinegar

sugar (see Method)

5 x 10 ml spoons/5 dessertspoons chopped mint

Put the apples in a preserving pan with the water and the mint. Simmer until the apples are soft and pulpy, then add the vinegar and boil for 5 minutes. Strain through a scalded jelly bag and leave to drip for 1 – 2 hours. Measure the juice and return it to the cleaned pan. Add 900 g/2 lb sugar for each 1.2 litres/2 pints of juice, and bring to the boil, stirring until the sugar is dissolved. Boil rapidly until setting point is nearly reached, add the chopped mint, then boil steadily until setting point is reached. Remove from the heat, pot and cover immediately. When cold, label and store.

BRANDIED PEARS

350 g/12 oz caster sugar

600 ml/1 pint water

900 g/2 lb English Conference *or* Comice pears, peeled, halved or quartered and cored

300 ml/¹/₂ pint brandy (approx)

Put the sugar and water into a pan, and cook, without stirring, until a syrup is formed. Add the fruit to the syrup, simmer gently and cook for 3 – 5 minutes, according to the ripeness of the fruit. Remove the pears from the syrup with a draining spoon, cool and pack neatly into clean, tested preserving jars with wide necks.
Boil the syrup to 110°C/230°F, then measure and add an equal quantity of brandy. Stir together well and pour over the fruit. Tap the jars to release any air bubbles, then seal and label. Store in a cool, dark place.

LEMON CURD

Yield 300 g/11 oz (approx)

grated rind and juice of 2 lemons
225 g/8 oz lump *or* granulated sugar
75 g/3 oz butter
3 eggs, lightly beaten

Put the lemon rind, juice and sugar into the top of a double boiler or basin over boiling water. Stir occasionally until the sugar dissolves. Remove from the heat and stir in the butter. Leave to cool. Pour the cooled mixture over the eggs, then strain it back into the pan or basin and place over gentle heat. Stir frequently with a wooden spoon until the mixture begins to thicken. When it coats the back of the spoon lightly, pour into small jars, taking care to fill to the brim. Cover and label.

LEFT Mincemeat

BELOW Lemon Curd

MINCEMEAT

Yield 1.8 kg/4 lb (approx)

225 g/8 oz cut mixed peel, finely chopped
225 g/8 oz seedless raisins, finely chopped
25 g/1 oz preserved stem ginger, finely chopped
225 g/8 oz cooking apples, peeled, cored and grated
225 g/8 oz shredded suet
225 g/8 oz sultanas
225 g/8 oz currants
225 g/8 oz soft brown sugar
50 g/2 oz blanched chopped almonds
a generous pinch each of mixed spice, ground ginger and ground cinnamon
grated rind and juice of 2 lemons and 1 orange
150 ml/¼ pint brandy

Combine all the ingredients thoroughly in a large basin. Leave, covered, for 2 days, in a cool place, stirring occasionally. (This prevents fermentation later.) Pot, cover and label. Store in a cool, dry place.

PEAR AND GINGER CHUTNEY

Yield 2.7 kg/6 lb (approx)

1.35 kg/3 lb hard pears, English Conference *or* Comice, cut into chunks
450 g/1 lb English dessert apples, cut into chunks
450 g/1 lb onions, skinned and sliced
75 g/3 oz preserved ginger, chopped
600 ml/1 pint cider vinegar
675 g/1½ lb brown sugar
1 x 2.5 ml spoon/½ teaspoon ground mace
6 cloves
1 x 2.5 ml spoon/½ teaspoon white pepper
1 x 2.5 ml spoon/½ teaspoon Cayenne pepper
50 g/2 oz salt
1 bay leaf
1 x 5 ml spoon/1 teaspoon allspice berries
1 x 5 ml spoon/1 teaspoon coriander seeds

Put the pears and apples, onions and ginger into a large pan, and add the vinegar. Bring to simmering point and simmer for 1 hour. Add the remaining ingredients and stir over gentle heat until the sugar is dissolved. Simmer steadily for another hour or until the mixture becomes fairly thick. Pot and cover, then cool, wipe the jars, label and store.

Bread and Butter Relish

BREAD AND BUTTER RELISH

2 cucumbers, thinly sliced
450 g/1 lb onions, thinly sliced
1 large green pepper, sliced
50 g/2 oz salt
450 g/1 lb caster sugar
1 x 2.5 ml spoon/½ teaspoon turmeric
1 x 2.5 ml spoon/½ teaspoon celery seed
1 x 5 ml spoon/1 teaspoon mustard seed
300 ml/½ pint cider vinegar
150 ml/¼ pint water

Put the vegetables into a large earthenware bowl and mix with the salt. Leave to stand for 3 hours, then rinse and drain well.
Mix together in a large saucepan the sugar, turmeric, celery and mustard seeds, vinegar and water. Bring to the boil and boil for 6 minutes. Add the drained vegetables and heat slowly to boiling point. Remove from the heat and pack into prepared jars. Seal at once with vinegar-proof covers.

BANANA CHUTNEY

Yield 2.7 kg/6 lb (approx)

30 bananas, sliced
65 g/2½ oz onions, sliced
25 – 50 g/1 – 2 oz fresh chillies, finely chopped
1.8 litres/3 pints white vinegar
225 g/8 oz seedless raisins
50 g/2 oz salt
50 g/2 oz ground ginger
450 g/1 lb brown sugar

Put all the ingredients into a saucepan and boil gently for 2 hours, stirring occasionally. When the chutney is of a good, thick consistency, pot and cover. Cool, wipe the jars, label and store.

PICCALILLI

900 g/2 lb prepared cauliflower, cucumber, shallots and broad beans, cut into small pieces
65 g/2½ oz cooking salt
900 ml/1½ pints vinegar
12 chillies
225 g/8 oz granulated sugar
25 g/1 oz dry mustard
15 g/½ oz turmeric
2 x 15 ml spoons/2 tablespoons cornflour

Put the vegetables into a large earthenware bowl and sprinkle with the cooking salt. Leave for 24 hours, then rinse and drain well.
Boil the vinegar and chillies for 2 minutes, leave to stand for 30 minutes, and then strain the vinegar. Mix together the sugar, mustard, turmeric and cornflour. Blend with a little of the cooled vinegar. Bring the rest of the vinegar back to the boil, pour it over the blended mixture, return to the saucepan and boil for 3 minutes. Remove from the heat and fold in the drained vegetables. Pack into prepared jars and seal at once with vinegar-proof covers.

APPLE CHUTNEY

Yield 4.5 kg/10 lb (approx)

2.4 litres/4 pints vinegar
1.35 kg/3 lb sugar
25 g/1 oz salt
1 x 5 ml spoon/1 teaspoon ground allspice
2.7 kg/6 lb apples, peeled, cored and chopped
350 g/12 oz preserved ginger, chopped
900 g/2 lb sultanas, chopped

Mix together the vinegar, sugar, salt and spice, and bring to the boil. Add the apples, and simmer for 10 minutes before adding the ginger and sultanas. Simmer until the mixture becomes fairly thick, then pot and cover. Cool, wipe the jars, label and store.

With all the fruit and vegetables around us, preserving time is an absolute delight

GREEN TOMATO CHUTNEY

Yield 2.7 kg/6 lb (approx)

1 x 15 ml spoon/1 tablespoon mustard seed
1 x 1.25 cm/½ inch piece ginger root
450 g/1 lb cooking apples, peeled, cored and chopped
450 g/1 lb onions, skinned and chopped
1.8 kg/4 lb green tomatoes, cut up roughly
450 g/1 lb sultanas
15 g/½ oz salt
½ x 2.5 ml spoon/¼ teaspoon Cayenne pepper
750 ml/1¼ pints malt vinegar
450 g/1 lb Demerara sugar

Tie the mustard seed and ginger root in a piece of muslin or thin cotton. Put with the apples, onions, tomatoes, sultanas, salt and Cayenne pepper in a large pan, and add just enough vinegar to cover.
Bring to simmering point and simmer for 20 minutes. Meanwhile, dissolve the sugar by warming it in the remaining vinegar. Add the mixture to the pan, and boil steadily until the chutney is a good, thick consistency. Pot and cover. Cool, wipe the jars, label and store.

GOOSEBERRY CHUTNEY

Yield 2.7 kg/6 lb (approx)

50 g/2 oz mustard seed
450 g/1 lb light soft brown sugar
1.8 litres/3 pints vinegar
450 g/1 lb onions, skinned and finely chopped
675 g/1½ lb seedless raisins
50 g/2 oz ground allspice
50 g/2 oz salt
1.8 kg/4 lb gooseberries, topped and tailed

Bruise the mustard seed gently. Mix the sugar with half the vinegar and boil until a syrup forms, then add the onions, raisins, spice and salt. Boil the gooseberries in the rest of the vinegar until tender, then mix in the sweet spiced vinegar, and cook until the chutney thickens. Pot and cover, then cool, wipe the jars and label. Store for 2 – 3 months if possible before use.

MUSTARD PICKLE

1.35 kg/3 lb prepared cucumber, beans, green tomatoes, onions, cauliflower and marrow, cut into small pieces
brine, using 225 g/8 oz salt for each 2.4 litres/ 4 pints water
25 g/1 oz plain flour
2 x 5 ml spoons/2 teaspoons turmeric
1 x 15 ml spoon/1 tablespoon dry mustard
900 ml/1½ pints white vinegar
125 g/5 oz caster sugar
1 x 5 ml spoon/1 teaspoon ground ginger

Put the vegetables into a large earthenware bowl and cover with the brine. Leave for 24 hours, then rinse and drain well.
Mix together the flour, turmeric and mustard, then blend with enough vinegar to make a thin paste. Simmer the vegetables for 20 minutes with the remaining vinegar, the sugar and ginger. Remove the vegetables with a draining spoon and pack into prepared jars. Add the blended flour mixture to the hot liquid and bring to the boil. Boil for 1 minute, then pour over the vegetables. Seal at once with vinegar-proof covers.

Mustard Pickle

PICKLED ONIONS

small even-sized onions

1 x 5 ml spoon/1 teaspoon salt (approx) for each
600 ml/1 pint water

cold spiced vinegar

Skin the onions with a stainless knife and drop
them into a basin of salted water until all have been
skinned. Remove from the water, and drain
thoroughly before packing into prepared jars or
bottles. Cover with the cold spiced vinegar and put
on vinegar-proof covers. Keep for at least a month
before using.

SPICED VINEGAR

7 g/¼ oz each, whole cloves, allspice, cinnamon,
white peppercorns and ginger

1.2 litres/2 pints malt, distilled *or* white vinegar

Put the ingredients in a heatproof bowl and cover
with a plate. Stand the bowl in a saucepan of cold
water, bring the water gently to the boil and draw
the pan off the heat. Leave for 2 hours, then strain.
Store in a sealed bottle.

PICKLED RED CABBAGE

1 medium-sized firm red cabbage, quartered and
shredded

salt

onions, very thinly sliced

soft brown sugar (light *or* dark)

cold spiced vinegar

Put layers of the cabbage into a large basin or dish,
sprinkling each layer with salt. Leave overnight.
Drain the cabbage very thoroughly in a
colander, pressing out all the surplus liquid.
Pack a layer of cabbage, about 7.5 cm/3 inches,
into large jars. Cover with a layer of very thinly
sliced onion, and sprinkle with 1 x 5 ml spoon/
1 teaspoon brown sugar. Add another 7.5 cm/
3 inches of cabbage, another layer of onion and
another spoon of sugar. Continue until the jars are
filled, ending with the onion and sugar. Cover with
the spiced vinegar, put on vinegar-proof covers and
leave for at least 5 – 7 days before opening.

PICKLED WALNUTS

soft green walnuts (picked before the shell has
begun to form)

brine, using 100 g/4 oz salt for each 1.2 litres/
2 pints water

hot spiced vinegar

Prick the walnuts well with a stainless fork; if the
shell can be felt, do not use the walnut. The shell
begins to form opposite the stalk, about 5 mm/
¼ inch from the end. Cover with the brine and
leave to soak for about 6 days.
Drain the walnuts, make fresh brine and leave to
soak for a further 7 days. Drain again, and spread
on a single layer of clean newspaper leaving the
walnuts exposed to the air, preferably in sunshine,
until they blacken (1 – 2 days). Pack into prepared
jars and cover with hot spiced vinegar. Put on
vinegar-proof covers when cold. Leave for at least a
month before using.

WORCESTERSHIRE SAUCE

Makes 1.5 litres/2½ pints (approx)

4 shallots, skinned and finely chopped

1.2 litres/2 pints good malt vinegar

6 x 15 ml spoons/6 tablespoons walnut ketchup

75 ml/3 fl oz anchovy essence

4 x 15 ml spoons/4 tablespoons soy sauce

1 x 2.5 ml spoon/½ teaspoon Cayenne pepper

salt

Put the ingredients into a large bottle, and cork it tightly. Shake well three or four times daily for about 14 days, then strain the sauce into small, prepared bottles, leaving a headspace. Cork tightly, label and store in a cool, dry place.

MINT VINEGAR

175 g/6 oz (approx) chopped young, fresh mint

25 g/1 oz sugar

600 ml/1 pint wine vinegar

If it is necessary to wash the mint, drain it before chopping. Sprinkle the mint with the sugar. Boil the vinegar, pour it over the mint, and then bottle. The mint will keep in the vinegar through the winter months, and the vinegar can be strained and used for salad dressings.

RASPBERRY VINEGAR

raspberries

white wine vinegar

water

caster sugar

Put the fruit into a basin. Cover with equal quantities of vinegar and water, then leave to stand overnight.
Strain off the liquid through a fine sieve or jelly bag. To each 300 ml/½ pint liquid, add 225 g/8 oz caster sugar. Pour into a saucepan and boil for 10 minutes. Pour the hot liquid into prepared bottles and seal at once. Label when cold. Diluted with water, this vinegar makes a cooling summer drink.

WALNUT KETCHUP

450 g/1 lb onions, skinned and chopped

2.4 litres/4 pints vinegar

225 g/8 oz salt

25 g/1 oz whole peppercorns

15 g/½ oz whole allspice berries

1 x 2.5 ml spoon/½ teaspoon whole cloves

1 x 2.5 ml spoon/½ teaspoon ground nutmeg

100 green walnuts (picked before the shell has hardened)

Boil all the ingredients together, except the walnuts. Wearing gloves to prevent staining your hands, cut up the walnuts, crush them, and put into a large pan or basin. Pour the boiling vinegar over them, and leave for 14 days, stirring daily. Strain off the liquid and simmer it in a pan for about an hour. Pour it into prepared bottles, leaving a headspace, and seal at once. Label when cold. Discard the crushed walnuts.

Cooking for the Festivals and Other Special Occasions

Christmas

MY TRADITIONAL ROAST TURKEY

1 x 5.4 kg/12 lb turkey
450 g/1 lb herb forcemeat (see page 52)
675 g/1½ lb seasoned sausage-meat
2 – 3 rashers fat bacon

Stuff the neck of the bird with the forcemeat and put the sausage-meat inside the body. Truss, and lay the bacon rashers over the breast. Roast in a hot oven, 220°C/425°F/Gas 7, for 15 – 20 minutes, then reduce the heat to moderate, 180°C/350°F/Gas 4, and cook for 4 hours and 20 minutes until tender, basting frequently. About 20 minutes before serving, remove the bacon to allow the breast to brown. Remove the trussing strings. Serve on a hot dish.

Serve with gravy, bacon rolls, grilled chipolata sausages, Bread Sauce (page 51) Cranberry Sauce and with roast potatoes and Brussels sprouts.

CRANBERRY SAUCE

Makes 375 ml/12 fl oz (approx)

150 ml/¼ pint water
175 g/6 oz sugar
225 g/8 oz cranberries
2 – 3 x 15 ml spoons/2 – 3 tablespoons sherry

Put the water and sugar in a saucepan and stir over gentle heat until the sugar dissolves. Add the cranberries and sherry, and cook gently for about 10 minutes until the cranberries have burst and are quite tender. Leave to cool.

My traditional Roast Turkey with all its trimmings

PAT AND JACK'S HONEY AND PINEAPPLE HAM

Serves 8 – 10

1.35 – 1.8 kg/3 – 4 lb parboiled York ham
600 ml/1 pint dry cider
4 x 5 ml spoons/4 teaspoons softened butter
1 x 15 ml spoon/1 tablespoon double cream

GARNISH

1 x 5 ml spoon/1 teaspoon mixed English mustard
3 x 15 ml spoons/3 tablespoons stiff honey
a good pinch of ground cloves
225 g/8 oz canned pineapple cubes
maraschino cherries, halved
watercress sprigs

Put the ham in a baking tin with the cider. Cover the tin tightly with foil. Bake the ham in a moderate oven, 180°C/350°F/Gas 4, for 30 minutes. Meanwhile, mix together the mustard, honey and cloves for the glaze. Drain the pineapple, reserving the juice.

When the ham is baked, remove the foil and pour off the cider into a measuring jug. Remove the rind. Score the fat in a pattern of 3.75 – 5 cm/1½ – 2 inch squares, then brush it all over with the mustard and honey glaze. Place pineapple pieces and halved cherries, cut side down, in alternate squares on the ham. Brush over with a little more glaze. Cook, loosely covered with the foil, in the oven for 20 – 30 minutes until the glaze is set.

Meanwhile, measure the cider and make it up to 600 ml/1 pint with the reserved pineapple juice, if required. Heat to simmering point in a saucepan. Stir in the butter, in small pieces, and melt. Simmer until well reduced and flavoured. Remove from the heat, and stir in the cream. Pour the sauce into a warmed sauce-boat and keep warm. Place the ham on a carving dish and garnish with watercress. Serve the sauce separately.

Pat and Jack's Honey and Pineapple Ham

MY MOTHER'S CHRISTMAS PUDDING

225 g/8 oz plain flour

a pinch of salt

1 x 5 ml spoon/1 teaspoon ground ginger

1 x 5 ml spoon/1 teaspoon mixed spice

1 x 5 ml spoon/1 teaspoon grated nutmeg

50 g/2 oz chopped blanched almonds

450 g/1 lb soft light *or* dark brown sugar

275 g/10 oz shredded suet

275 g/10 oz sultanas

275 g/10 oz currants

225 g/8 oz seedless raisins

225 g/8 oz cut mixed peel

200 g/7 oz stale white breadcrumbs

6 eggs

75 ml/3 fl oz stout

juice of 1 orange

50 ml/2 fl oz brandy *or* to taste

150 – 300 ml/¼ – ½ pint milk

Sift together the flour, salt, ginger, mixed spice and nutmeg into a mixing bowl. Add the almonds, sugar, suet, sultanas, currants, raisins, peel and breadcrumbs. Beat together the eggs, stout, orange juice, brandy and 150 ml/¼ pint milk. Stir this into the dry ingredients, adding more milk if required, to give a soft dropping consistency. Put the mixture into four 600 ml/1 pint prepared basins, cover with greased paper or foil, and a floured cloth. Put into deep boiling water and boil steadily for 6 – 7 hours, or half steam for the same length of time.

To store, cover with a clean dry cloth, wrap in greaseproof paper and store in a cool place until required. To re-heat, boil or steam for 1½ – 2 hours.

Serve with Brandy Butter.

BRANDY BUTTER

Makes 175 g/6 oz (approx)

50 g/2 oz butter

100 g/4 oz caster sugar

1 – 2 x 15 ml spoons/1 – 2 tablespoons brandy

Cream the butter and sugar until pale and light. Work in the brandy, a little at a time, taking care not to allow the mixture to curdle. Chill before using. If the mixture has separated slightly after standing, beat well before serving.

My mother's Christmas Pudding

MY GRANDMOTHER'S CHRISTMAS CAKE

225 g/8 oz plain flour

½ × 2.5 ml spoon/¼ teaspoon salt

1 – 2 × 5 ml spoons/1 – 2 teaspoons mixed spice

225 g/8 oz butter

225 g/8 oz caster sugar

6 eggs

2 – 4 × 15 ml spoons/2 – 4 tablespoons brandy

100 g/4 oz glacé cherries, cut up

50 g/2 oz preserved ginger, chopped

50 g/2 oz walnuts, chopped

225 g/8 oz currants

225 g/8 oz sultanas

175 g/6 oz seedless raisins

75 g/3 oz mixed peel

COATING AND ICING

almond paste

royal icing (see page 84)

Grease and line a 20 cm/8 inch cake tin with doubled greaseproof paper and tie a strip of brown paper round the outside.
Sift together the flour, salt and spice. Cream together the butter and sugar until light and fluffy. Gradually beat in the eggs and the brandy. Stir the cherries, ginger, walnuts, dried fruit, peel and the flour into the creamed mixture. Put into the tin and make a slight hollow in the centre. Bake in a warm oven, 160°C/325°F/Gas 3, for 45 minutes, reduce the heat to cool, 150°C/300°F/Gas 2, and bake for a further hour. Reduce the heat to very cool, 140°C/275°F/Gas 1, and continue cooking for 45 minutes – 1 hour until firm to the touch. Cool in the tin. Cover with almond paste and decorate with royal icing.

ALMOND PASTE

For the top and sides of a 20 cm/8 inch cake
Makes 675 g/1½ lb (approx)

350 g/12 oz ground almonds

350 g/12 oz icing sugar

2 egg yolks *or* 2 egg whites

almond essence to taste

Work all the ingredients together to make a pliable paste. Handle it as little as possible, as the warmth of the hands draws out the oil from the ground almonds.

THE FAMILY'S TWELFTH NIGHT CAKE

175 g/6 oz margarine

75 g/3 oz soft dark brown sugar

3 eggs

350 g/12 oz plain flour

4 × 15 ml spoons/4 tablespoons milk

1 × 5 ml spoon/1 teaspoon bicarbonate of soda

2 × 15 ml spoons/2 tablespoons golden syrup

1 × 2.5 ml spoon/½ teaspoon mixed spice

1 × 2.5 ml spoon/½ teaspoon ground cinnamon

a pinch of salt

50 g/2 oz currants

100 g/4 oz sultanas

100 g/4 oz cut mixed peel

1 dried bean

1 large dried whole pea

Cream the fat and sugar until light and fluffy. Beat in the eggs, one at a time, adding a little flour with each. Warm the milk. Dissolve the bicarbonate of soda in the warmed milk and add the syrup. Mix the spices and salt with the remaining flour. Add this to the creamed mixture alternately with the milk mixture. Mix in the dried fruit and peel lightly until evenly blended. Place half the cake mixture in a greased and lined 15 cm/6 inch round cake tin, lay the bean and pea in the centre, then cover with the rest of the cake mixture. Bake in a moderate oven, 180°C/350°F/Gas 4, for about 2 hours.

SANDIE'S MINCE PIES

Makes 12

450 g/1 lb prepared flaky, rough puff *or* puff pastry
(see pages 38 and 44)

225 g/8 oz mincemeat

25 g/1 oz caster *or* icing sugar for dredging

Roll out the pastry 2.5 mm/⅛ inch thick on a
lightly floured surface, and use just over half to line
twelve 7.5 cm/3 inch patty tins. Cut out 12 lids
from the rest of the pastry. Place a spoonful of
mincemeat in each pastry case. Dampen the edges
of the cases and cover with the pastry lids. Seal the
edges well, brush the tops with water, and dredge
with the sugar. Make two small cuts in the top of
each pie, and bake in a very hot oven,
230°C/450°F/Gas 8, for 15 – 20 minutes or until
golden-brown.
Serve with Brandy Butter (page 105).

Sandie's Mince Pies

Shrove Tuesday

LEMON PANCAKES

Makes 8

100 g/4 oz plain flour, sifted

½ × 2.5 ml spoon/¼ teaspoon salt

1 egg

2 × 5 ml spoons/2 teaspoons caster sugar

300 ml/½ pint milk

oil

lemon juice

extra caster sugar

Mix the flour and salt in a mixing bowl, make a
well in the centre and add the egg and the sugar.
Stir in half the milk, and beat vigorously until the
mixture is smooth and bubbly, then stir in the rest
of the milk. Pour the batter into a jug.
Heat a little oil in an omelet pan. Pour off any
excess, as the pan should only be coated with a thin
film of grease. Stir the batter and pour in
2 – 3 × 15 ml spoons/2 – 3 tablespoons batter (just
enough to cover the base of the pan thinly). Tilt
and rotate the pan to ensure that the batter runs
over the whole surface evenly. Cook over moderate
heat for about 1 minute until the pancake is set and
golden-brown underneath. Toss or turn the
pancake with a palette knife, and cook the second
side for about 30 seconds until golden. Slide out on
to sugared paper, sprinkle with lemon juice, roll up
and sprinkle with extra caster sugar. Repeat this
process until all the batter has been used, greasing
the pan when necessary.
Serve the pancakes accompanied by lemon
wedges.

Easter

EASTER BISCUITS

| 225 g/8 oz plain flour |
| 1 x 2.5 ml spoon /¹/₂ teaspoon ground cinnamon |
| ¹/₂ x 2.5 ml spoon/¹/₄ teaspoon salt |
| 100 – 175 g/4 – 6 oz butter *or* margarine |
| 100 – 175 g/4 – 6 oz caster sugar |
| 1 egg yolk *or* ¹/₂ beaten egg |
| 50 g/2 oz currants |
| beaten egg white |
| caster sugar for dredging |

Hot Cross Buns and *Easter Biscuits*

Mix together the flour, cinnamon and salt. Cream the fat and sugar until light and fluffy, then beat in the egg. Fold in the flour and currants, using a knife and then the fingers. On a lightly floured surface, knead lightly and roll out to 5 mm – 1.25 cm/¹/₄ – ¹/₂ inch thick. Cut into rounds with a 6.25 – 7.5 cm/2¹/₂ – 3 inch cutter. Re-roll and re-cut any trimmings. Prick the surface of the biscuits in two or three places with a fork, then place on a well greased baking sheet. Bake in a moderate oven, 180°C/350°F/Gas 4, for 10 – 15 minutes. Brush with beaten egg white and sprinkle with caster sugar, then bake for another 5 minutes. Leave on the baking sheet for 5 minutes before transferring to a wire rack. Store in an airtight tin when cold.

HOT CROSS BUNS

Makes 12

450 g/1 lb strong white flour
1 x 5 ml spoon/1 teapoon sugar
175 ml/6 fl oz milk
100 ml/4 fl oz warm water
25 g/1 oz fresh yeast *or* 1 x 15 ml spoon/ 1 tablespoon dried yeast
3 x 2.5 ml spoons/1½ teaspoons mixed spice
1 x 2.5 ml spoon/½ teaspoon ground cinnamon
1 x 2.5 ml spoon/½ teaspoon grated nutmeg
1 x 5 ml spoon/1 teaspoon salt
50 g/2 oz butter
90 g/3½ oz caster sugar
100 g/4 oz currants
50 g/2 oz chopped mixed peel
1 egg

Sift about 75 g/3 oz of the flour and the sugar into a large bowl. Warm 150 ml/¼ pint milk until hand-hot. Add 75 ml/3 fl oz water to the milk and blend in the fresh yeast or sprinkle on the dried yeast. Pour the yeast liquid into the flour and sugar, and beat well. Leave the bowl in a warm place for 20 minutes. Sift the rest of the flour, the spices and the salt into a bowl. Rub in the butter. Add 50 g/2 oz caster sugar and the dried fruit. Beat the egg into the frothy yeast mixture and add the flour, fat and fruit mixture. Mix to a very soft dough, then knead for about 5 minutes on a lightly floured surface until the dough is smooth and no longer sticky. Place in a large, lightly oiled polythene bag and leave in a warm place for about 1 hour or until the dough has almost doubled in size.

Knead the dough again until firm, then cut into 12 equal pieces and shape each into a round bun. Place on a floured baking sheet, leaving plenty of space between each bun. With a sharp knife, slash a cross on the top of each bun, or make crosses with pastry trimmings. Cover with polythene and leave for about 35 minutes until the dough has doubled in size. Bake in a hot oven, 220°C/425°F/Gas 7, for about 15 – 20 minutes until golden-brown.

Glaze the hot buns by boiling together the remaining milk, water and sugar for 6 minutes and brushing the surface of each bun with the glaze.

SIMNEL CAKE

Dundee Cake mixture (see page 78)

DECORATION

450 g/1 lb almond paste (see page 106)
apricot jam
1 egg, beaten
50 g/2 oz prepared white glacé icing (see page 85)
Easter decorations

Prepare the Dundee cake recipe. Put half the mixture into the lined 17.5 cm/7 inch tin. Cut off one-third of the almond paste and roll it into a 17.5 cm/7 inch round about 1.25 cm/½ inch thick. Place it on the cake mixture lightly, and put the remaining cake mixture on top. Bake in a moderate oven, 180°C/350°F/Gas 4, for 1 hour, reduce the heat to warm, 160°C/325°F/Gas 3, and bake for a further 1½ hours. Cool in the tin, then turn on to a wire rack.

Warm, then sieve the apricot jam. When the cake is cold, divide the remaining almond paste into two equal portions. Roll one-half into a 17.5 cm/7 inch round. Brush the top of the cake with the apricot jam and press the almond paste lightly on to it. Trim the edge neatly. Make small balls from the remaining paste (11 is the traditional number), and place them round the edge of the cake. Brush the balls with beaten egg and brown under the grill. Pour glacé icing into the centre of the cake and decorate with chickens and Easter eggs.

Simnel Cake

Harvest Festival

SANDIE'S WALNUT TEABREAD

350 g/12 oz self-raising flour

1 x 2.5 ml spoon/½ teaspoon salt

75 g/3 oz caster sugar

50 g/2 oz walnut halves

2 eggs, beaten

2 x 15 ml spoons/2 tablespoons clear honey

150 ml/¼ pint milk

50 g/2 oz butter, melted

DECORATION

100 g/4 oz prepared glacé icing (see page 85)

Sift together the flour, salt and sugar into a bowl.
Reserve four pieces of walnut for decoration, and
finely chop the remainder. Mix this into the flour
mixture. Make a well in the centre and add the
eggs, honey, milk and melted butter; mix until well
blended. Pour into a greased 900 g/2 lb loaf tin and
bake in a warm oven, 160°C/325°F/Gas 3, for
1½ hours. Cool on a wire rack.
To decorate, pour the icing over the top of the
teabread, allowing it to trickle down the sides.
Roughly chop the reserved walnut pieces and use
to decorate the top.

MY HARVEST ROLLS

risen Farmhouse Bread dough (see page 72)

milk *or* flour

Divide the dough into 50 g/2 oz pieces, and shape
as follows:
Divide the pieces equally into three. Shape each
piece into a ball and arrange on a greased baking
sheet in the shape of a cloverleaf, pressing lightly
together.
Roll each of the remaining pieces into strands
approximately 12.5 cm/5 inches long. Knot loosely
and place on another greased baking sheet.
Brush the rolls with milk or dust with flour, then
cover with oiled polythene, and leave in a warm
place until doubled in size. Remove the polythene,
and bake in a hot oven, 220°C/425°F/Gas 7, for
about 20 minutes, until golden-brown.

*Sandie's Walnut Teabread, Dolly's Treacle and Ginger
Loaf, Pat's Cheesy Tomato Loaf and my Harvest Rolls*

PAT'S CHEESY TOMATO LOAF

675 g/1½ lb strong white flour
15 g/½ oz salt
15 g/½ oz lard
15 g/½ oz fresh yeast *or* 2 × 5 ml spoons/2 teaspoons dried yeast and 1 × 5 ml spoon/1 teaspoon sugar
300 ml/½ pint warm water
125 g/5 oz concentrated tomato purée
100 g/4 oz Cheddar cheese, grated
milk

Sift together the flour and salt into a large bowl, and rub in the lard. Blend the fresh yeast with half the warm water or reconstitute the dried yeast. Blend the tomato purée with the remaining water. Pour the yeast and tomato liquids into the dry ingredients and knead for about 10 minutes to form a smooth dough. Place in a large, lightly oiled polythene bag and leave in a warm place until doubled in size.

Turn the dough on to a lightly floured surface, flatten it, then incorporate half the cheese by kneading it in. Divide into twelve equal-sized pieces, and shape each piece into a smooth ball. Arrange five dough balls in each of two greased 15 cm/6 inch sandwich tins to form a ring. Place the two remaining balls in the centre of each tin and brush with milk. Cover with the oiled polythene and leave to rise for about 30 minutes until doubled in size, then remove the polythene.

Bake in a hot oven, 220°C/425°F/Gas 7, for 20 minutes, then sprinkle the remaining cheese on top of each loaf, and bake for another 10 – 15 minutes.

DOLLY'S TREACLE AND GINGER LOAF

225 g/8 oz wholewheat flour
225 g/8 oz strong white flour
2 × 5 ml spoons/2 teaspoons salt
2 × 5 ml spoons/2 teaspoons sugar
15 g/½ oz lard
15 g/½ oz fresh yeast *or* 2 × 5 ml spoons/2 teaspoons dried yeast
300 ml/½ pint warm water
2 × 15 ml spoons/2 tablespoons black treacle
25 g/1 oz margarine
2 × 5 ml spoons/2 teaspoons ground ginger
50 g/2 oz currants

GLAZE

2 × 15 ml spoons/2 tablespoons orange jelly marmalade

Sift together the flours, salt and sugar into a large bowl, and rub in the lard. Blend the fresh yeast into the water or reconstitute the dried yeast. Add the yeast liquid to the flour, and mix to a dough that leaves the bowl clean. Turn on to a lightly floured surface and knead thoroughly until smooth, then place in a large, lightly oiled polythene bag, and leave in a warm place until doubled in size.

Replace the dough in the bowl and add the remaining ingredients. Squeeze all the ingredients together until the mixture is no longer streaky. Form the dough into a loaf shape and place in a greased 450 g/1 lb loaf tin. Place the tin in the greased polythene bag and leave for about 1 hour in a warm place until it is within 1.25 cm/½ inch of the top of the tin.

Remove from the bag and bake in a fairly hot oven, 200°C/400°F/Gas 6, for 40 minutes, then cool.

To glaze, heat the marmalade gently in a small pan and use it to brush the top of the loaf. Serve sliced, with butter.

Entertaining

PAT'S LIVER PÂTÉ

Serves 4 – 6

75 g/3 oz butter
225 g/8 oz pig's liver, chopped
225 g/8 oz poultry livers, chopped
100 g/4 oz very lean ham *or* bacon, chopped
1 small onion, chopped
a few gherkins, chopped
1 – 2 hard-boiled eggs, chopped
salt and pepper
1 – 2 x 5 ml spoons/1 – 2 teaspoons dried mixed herbs
melted clarified butter

Melt the butter in a pan and cook the meats and onion for 5 – 6 minutes. Mince finely twice to make a smooth paste. Add the gherkins and the eggs, together with the seasoning and herbs. Put into an ovenproof terrine or similar dish and cover with buttered greaseproof paper. Stand the dish in a pan of hot water which comes half-way up the sides. Cook in a moderate oven, 180°C/350°F/Gas 4, for about 30 minutes.

When cooked, either cover immediately with a layer of clarified butter and leave to cool, then chill before serving; or place under a light weight and cover with clarified butter as soon as cold. Serve the pâté in the dish in which it has been cooked, or cut it into slices and place on a bed of crisp lettuce. Serve with warm Melba toast.

DOLLY'S SMOKED MACKEREL PÂTÉ

Serves 4 – 6

2 whole hot-smoked mackerel, skinned, boned and flaked
50 g/2 oz softened butter
1 clove of garlic, crushed
1 x 15 ml spoon/1 tablespoon lemon juice
salt and freshly ground black pepper
melted clarified butter

GARNISH

stuffed olives, sliced
bay leaves

Put the fish into a bowl, add the butter and garlic, and pound well. Stir in the lemon juice, and season to taste. Put into a suitable dish and cover with clarified butter. Leave until the butter is firm, then garnish with sliced olives and bay leaves. Serve with warm Melba toast.

Dolly's Smoked Mackerel Pâté

MY OWN CROWN ROAST OF LAMB

Serves 6

2 best ends of neck of lamb (6 cutlets each)
oil for brushing
salt and pepper

SAFFRON RICE

600 ml/1 pint chicken stock
1/2 x 2.5 ml spoon/1/4 teaspoon powdered saffron
50 g/2 oz butter
1 stick of celery, chopped
1 medium-sized onion, chopped
175 g/6 oz long-grain white rice
4 x 15 ml spoons/4 tablespoons dry white wine
25 g/1 oz blanched almonds, chopped
2 dessert apples, peeled, cored and chopped
50 g/2 oz frozen green peas

Remove the fat and meat from the top 5 cm/ 2 inches of the thin ends of the bones and scrape the bone ends clean. Slice the lower half of each best end of neck between each bone, about two-thirds up from the base. Trim off any excess fat. Turn the joints so that the bones are on the outside and the meat is on the inside, and sew the pieces together with a trussing needle and fine string. The thick ends of the meat will be the base of the crown, so make sure they stand level.

Place the prepared crown roast in a roasting tin. Brush it with oil and season well with salt and pepper. Wrap a piece of foil round the top of each cutlet bone to prevent it from scorching. Cook in a fairly hot oven, 190°C/375°F/Gas 5, for 1/4 – 1 1/2 hours.

About 30 minutes before the end of the cooking time, make the saffron rice. Heat the chicken stock in a saucepan with the powdered saffron. Heat 25 g/1 oz of the butter in a saucepan and fry the celery and onion gently until softened but not browned. Stir the rice into the vegetables and cook for 1 – 2 minutes. Pour on the wine and cook gently until the rice has absorbed it. Add 300 ml/1/2 pint of the hot stock and cook, uncovered, stirring occasionally, until almost all the liquid is absorbed. Pour the remaining stock into the rice and cook gently until it has been completely absorbed and the rice is just tender. Remove the rice from the heat and add the almonds, apples, peas and remaining butter. Cover the pan with a tight-fitting lid, and leave to cook in its own steam until the peas are thawed and heated through, and the roast is ready.

When cooked, place the crown roast on a warmed serving dish. Remove the foil from the cutlet bones. Fill the hollow centre of the roast with the hot saffron rice. Top each cutlet with a cutlet frill and serve. Any extra rice can be served separately.

My own Crown Roast of Lamb

My special Saddle of Lamb

MY SPECIAL SADDLE OF LAMB

Serves 6 – 8

1 saddle of lamb, boned (2.7 kg/6 lb approx)

salt and pepper

25 g/1 oz butter

1 onion, diced

175 g/6 oz oatmeal

1 x 5 ml spoon/1 teaspoon dried thyme

400 g/14 oz canned apricots, chopped and drained (juice reserved)

Season the cavity left by the removal of the saddle bone with salt and pepper. (A butcher will usually do this for you if you give him sufficient notice.) Melt the butter in a pan and fry the onion until soft. Stir in the oatmeal, thyme, apricots and 2 x 15 ml spoons/2 tablespoons of the reserved apricot juice. Mix thoroughly. Spoon the stuffing into the cavity, roll the saddle up and tie securely with string. Place in a roasting tin and cook in a moderate oven, 180°C/350°F/Gas 4, for 35 minutes to each 450 g/1 lb (weighed when stuffed). Ten minutes before the cooking time is complete, brush the saddle with the remaining apricot juice. Allow to rest before carving.

DOLLY'S BOEUF BOURGUIGNONNE

Serves 4 – 6

550 g/1¼ lb chuck steak, cut into 2.5 cm/1 inch cubes

300 ml/½ pint red wine

½ x 2.5 ml spoon/¼ teaspoon black pepper

1 x 2.5 ml spoon/½ teaspoon salt

bouquet garni

1 small onion, finely sliced

1 small carrot, finely sliced

2 cloves garlic, crushed

3 x 15 ml spoons/3 tablespoons oil

2 rashers bacon, without rinds and cut into small pieces

12 small onions

12 button mushrooms

25 g/1 oz flour

salt and pepper

300 ml/½ pint (approx) brown stock (see page 19)

GARNISH

sippets of fried bread

chopped parsley

Put the steak in a basin, pour the wine over it, and add the pepper, salt and bouquet garni. Add the onion, carrot and garlic, cover and leave to marinate for about 6 hours.
Heat most of the oil in a frying pan, add the bacon, and fry lightly, then remove and put to one side. Fry the onions and the mushrooms in the oil for 3 – 4 minutes, then remove and put to one side. Drain the meat, reserving the marinade, and pat dry on soft kitchen paper. Season the flour with salt and pepper and coat the meat in the flour. Add a little more oil to the frying pan and fry the meat until sealed all over. Put into an ovenproof casserole, then stir in the bacon, onions and mushrooms. Strain the marinade over the meat and add about 300 ml/½ pint stock. Cover and cook in a warm oven, 160°C/325°F/Gas 3, for about 2 hours. Season to taste. Serve garnished with sippets and chopped parsley.

MY SPECIAL ROAST LOIN OF PORK

Serves 6 – 7

1.35 kg/3 lb loin of pork on the bone

1 x 15 ml spoon/1 tablespoon finely chopped onion

1 x 2.5 ml spoon/½ teaspoon dried sage

1 x 2.5 ml spoon/½ teaspoon salt

½ x 2.5 ml spoon/¼ teaspoon freshly ground pepper

a pinch of dry mustard

smooth apricot jam

Ask the butcher to chine the pork and score the rind in narrow lines, or do it yourself with a sharp knife. Mix the onion with the sage, salt, pepper and mustard. Rub the mixture well into the surface of the meat. Roast the pork in a hot oven, 220°C/425°F/Gas 7, for 10 minutes, then reduce the heat to moderate, 180°C/350°F/Gas 4, for the rest of the calculated cooking time, allowing 30 minutes for each 450 g/1 lb plus 30 minutes extra. About 30 minutes before serving, cover with the jam, and continue cooking to crisp the crackling.
Serve with hot Apple Sauce (see page 46) and Gravy.

GRAVY

Makes 300 ml/½ pint (approx)

pan juices from roasting a joint of pork

1 x 15 ml spoon/1 tablespoon plain flour

300 ml/½ pint hot basic stock (see page 13)

salt and pepper

Pour off most of the fat from the roasting tin, leaving 2 x 15 ml spoons/2 tablespoons fat and sediment in the pan. Sift the flour over the fat and blend thoroughly with the pan juices. Stir and cook until browned. Gradually add the stock, and stir until boiling. Boil for 3 – 4 minutes, then season to taste. Strain, and serve very hot.

PAT'S SPECIAL GUARD OF HONOUR

Serves 6

2 best ends of neck of lamb (6 – 7 cutlets each)
2 x 15 ml spoons/2 tablespoons oil

STUFFING

25 g/1 oz butter *or* margarine
1 small onion
50 g/2 oz mushrooms
100 g/4 oz soft white breadcrumbs
1 x 15 ml spoon/1 tablespoon chopped parsley
grated rind of 1 lemon
salt and pepper
1 egg, beaten
milk

GRAVY

1 x 15 ml spoon/1 tablespoon plain flour
300 ml/½ pint vegetable stock (see page 54)
salt and pepper
gravy browning (optional)

GARNISH

parsley sprigs

Ask the butcher to chine the joints. Remove the fat and meat from the top 5 cm/2 inches of the thin end of the bones and scrape the bone ends clean. Wipe the meat and score the fat with a sharp knife in a lattice pattern. Place the joints together to form an arch.
Make the stuffing. Melt the butter or margarine in a frying pan and fry the onion gently for 5 minutes until softened but not browned. Mix together the fried onion, mushrooms, breadcrumbs, parsley, lemon rind and seasoning to taste. Add the egg to the stuffing with enough milk to bind it together. Stuff the cavity of the Guard of Honour.
Close the joints together at the top, by criss-crossing the bones. Cover the bones with foil to prevent them from scorching. Heat the oil in a baking tin and put in the Guard of Honour. Cook in a fairly hot oven, 190°C/375°F/Gas 5, for 1¼ – 1½ hours or until the lamb is tender. When cooked, transfer to a warmed serving dish, and allow to rest in the turned-off oven.
Meanwhile, make the gravy. Pour off most of the fat from the roasting tin. Stir in the flour, and cook gently for a few minutes. Gradually add the stock and stir until boiling. Reduce the heat and simmer for 2 minutes. Season to taste and add gravy browning, if liked. Pour into a warmed gravy-boat.
Remove the foil from the bones of the Guard of Honour and replace with cutlet frills. Garnish with sprigs of parsley.

PAT'S CHICKEN CHASSEUR

Serves 4 – 6

25 g/1 oz flour
salt and pepper
1 roasting chicken, divided into 8 serving portions
1 x 15 ml spoon/1 tablespoon cooking oil
50 g/2 oz butter
25 g/1 oz onion *or* shallot, chopped
175 g/6 oz button mushrooms, sliced
150 ml/¼ pint dry white wine
3 tomatoes, chopped
300 ml/½ pint chicken stock
1 sprig each of fresh tarragon, chervil and parsley, chopped

Season the flour with salt and pepper, and use to dust the chicken portions. Heat the oil and butter in a frying pan, and fry the chicken pieces until tender and browned all over, allowing 15 – 20 minutes for dark meat (drumsticks and thighs), 10 – 12 minutes for light meat (breast and wings). When tender, remove from the pan, drain on soft kitchen paper, and transfer to a warmed serving dish. Cover loosely with buttered paper and keep hot.
Put the onion or shallot into the pan, in the fat in which the chicken was cooked, and fry gently without colouring. Add the mushrooms to the pan, and continue frying until tender. Pour in the wine, and add the chopped tomatoes and the stock. Stir until well blended, then simmer gently for 10 minutes. Add most of the herbs to the sauce and season to taste.
Pour the sauce over the chicken, sprinkle with the remaining herbs, and serve very hot.

Dolly's Coq au Vin

DOLLY'S COQ AU VIN

Serves 4 – 6

1 chicken, jointed with giblets
bouquet garni
salt and pepper
50 g/2 oz unsalted butter
1 x 15 ml spoon/1 tablespoon oil
125 g/5 oz green bacon rashers, rinds removed and chopped
125 g/5 oz button onions
2 x 15 ml spoons/2 tablespoons brandy
600 ml/1 pint Burgundy *or* other red wine
175 g/6 oz button mushrooms
1 clove of garlic, crushed
2 x 5 ml spoons/2 teaspoons concentrated tomato purée
25 g/1 oz butter
25 g/1 oz plain flour

GARNISH

croûtes of fried bread
chopped parsley

Place the giblets in a saucepan, cover with water, and add the bouquet garni, salt and pepper. Cook gently for 1 hour to make stock.

Heat the unsalted butter and the oil in a flameproof casserole, add the bacon and the onions, and cook slowly until the fat runs and the onions are lightly coloured. Remove them to a plate.

Brown the chicken lightly all over in the same fat, then pour off any surplus fat. Warm the brandy, set alight, and pour it over the chicken. When the flame dies down, add the wine, stock, bacon, onions, mushrooms, garlic and tomato purée. Cover with a lid and cook in a cool oven, 150°C/300°F/Gas 2, for 1 hour or until the chicken is tender.

Transfer the chicken to a serving dish and keep hot. Using a perforated spoon, remove the onions, bacon and mushrooms, and arrange over the chicken. Simmer the liquid until reduced by about one-third. Meanwhile, make a beurre manié by kneading together the 25 g/1 oz butter and flour. Lower the heat of the liquid to below boiling point and gradually whisk in the beurre manié in small pieces. Continue to whisk until the sauce thickens. Pour it over the chicken. Arrange croûtes of fried bread round the dish and sprinkle with chopped parsley.

MY ROAST GOOSE WITH FRUIT STUFFING AND RED CABBAGE

Serves 6 – 8

| 350 g/12 oz prunes |
| 1 goose with giblets |
| 1.8 litres/3 pints water |
| ½ lemon |
| salt and pepper |
| 450 g/1 lb cooking apples, peeled, cored and roughly chopped |
| 1 x 15 ml spoon/1 tablespoon redcurrant jelly |

RED CABBAGE

| 50 g/2 oz butter |
| 50 g/2 oz Demerara sugar |
| 1.35 kg/3 lb red cabbage, finely shredded |
| 75 ml/3 fl oz water |
| 75 ml/3 fl oz cider vinegar |
| salt and pepper |

Soak the prunes overnight. Remove the giblets from the goose and simmer them in the water until the liquid is reduced by half. Weigh the goose and calculate the cooking time at 20 minutes for each 450 g/1 lb. Remove the excess fat usually found around the vent. Rinse the inside of the bird, then rub the skin with lemon. Season with salt and pepper. Remove the stones from the prunes and chop the flesh. Mix the apples with the prunes and season to taste. Stuff into the body of the bird.

Place in a very hot oven, 230°C/450°F/Gas 8, reduce the temperature immediately to moderate, 180°C/350°F/Gas 4, and cook for the calculated time.

Meanwhile, prepare the red cabbage. Melt the butter in a large flameproof casserole. Add the sugar and cabbage, and stir well. Add the water, vinegar and seasoning, cover and cook in the bottom of the oven for about 2 hours, stirring occasionally.

When the goose is cooked, drain off the excess fat, retaining the juices in the pan. Add the redcurrant jelly and stir until it melts.

Serve the gravy and red cabbage separately.

ROAST STUFFED PHEASANT

I cook this for guests—Seth somehow always manages to get me some beautiful pheasants!

Serves 6

| 2 pheasants |
| ½ onion |
| 50 g/2 oz butter |

STUFFING

| 25 g/1 oz butter *or* margarine |
| 100 g/4 oz onion, finely chopped |
| 100 g/4 oz mushrooms, chopped |
| 50 g/2 oz ham, chopped |
| 75 g/3 oz soft white breadcrumbs |
| salt and pepper |
| 1 x 15 ml spoon/1 tablespoon stock (optional) |

GARNISH

| watercress sprigs |
| French dressing |

Wash the pheasant giblets, cover with cold water, add the half onion, and simmer gently for 40 minutes to make stock for the gravy.

Make the stuffing. Melt the butter or margarine and cook the onion until soft. Add the mushrooms and cook for a few minutes, then add the ham and the breadcrumbs. Stir, add salt and pepper, and the stock if the stuffing is too crumbly.

Divide the stuffing between the birds, filling the body cavities only. Truss the birds neatly and put in a roasting tin; spread with the butter. Roast in a fairly hot oven, 190°C/375°F/Gas 5, for 45 minutes – 1 hour, depending on the size of the birds; baste occasionally while roasting. Transfer the birds to a heated serving dish, and remove the trussing strings. Garnish with watercress tossed very lightly in French dressing.

Serve with Gravy (page 116), Bread Sauce (page 51) and fried breadcrumbs.

DOLLY'S SAVARIN

Serves 6 – 8

75 ml/3 fl oz milk
15 g/¹/₂ oz fresh yeast *or* 1 × 10 ml spoon/ 1 dessertspoon dried yeast
175 g/6 oz strong white flour
¹/₂ × 2.5 ml spoon/¹/₄ teaspoon salt
1 × 10 ml spoon/1 dessertspoon sugar
75 g/3 oz butter
3 eggs

RUM SYRUP

75 g/3 oz lump sugar
150 ml/¹/₄ pint water
2 × 15 ml spoons/2 tablespoons rum
1 × 15 ml spoon/1 tablespoon lemon juice

GLAZE

3 × 15 ml spoons/3 tablespoons apricot jam
2 × 15 ml spoons/2 tablespoons water

Warm the milk until tepid. Blend in the fresh yeast or sprinkle on the dried yeast. Stir in 25 g/1 oz of the flour and leave in a warm place for 20 minutes. Sift the rest of the flour, the salt and the sugar into a bowl. Rub in the butter. Add the yeast to the mixture, then add the eggs and beat until well mixed. Pour the mixture into an oiled 20 cm/8 inch ring mould, cover with a large, lightly oiled polythene bag, and leave in a warm place until the mixture has almost reached the top of the tin. Bake in a fairly hot oven, 200°C/400°F/Gas 6, for about 20 minutes or until golden-brown and springy to the touch.

To make the rum syrup, put the sugar and water in a pan and heat until the sugar has dissolved. Bring to the boil and boil steadily for 8 minutes. Add the rum and lemon juice. Turn the warm savarin on to a serving dish, prick all over with a fine skewer, and spoon the rum syrup over it.

To make the glaze, sieve the apricot jam into a saucepan, add the water and bring to the boil, stirring all the time. Brush the glaze all over the soaked savarin.

MY ORANGES IN CARAMEL SAUCE

Serves 4

6 oranges
300 ml/¹/₂ pint water
225 g/8 oz sugar
25 – 50 ml/1 – 2 fl oz chilled orange juice

Pare the rind carefully from one of the oranges, and cut it into thin strips. Soak in 150 ml/¹/₄ pint of the water for 1 hour, then simmer gently for 20 minutes. Drain. Peel and remove the white pith from all the oranges, and cut the flesh into 5 mm/ ¹/₄ inch thick slices. Place in a glass serving dish. Put the sugar and the remaining water into a pan. Heat gently, stirring until the sugar has dissolved, then boil rapidly until it is a golden caramel colour. Draw off the heat immediately and add enough orange juice to give the consistency of sauce required. Replace over the heat, stir until just blended, then add the drained orange rind. Pour the caramel sauce over the oranges and chill for at least 3 hours before serving.

My Oranges in Caramel Sauce

PAT'S APRICOT AND ALMOND TART

Serves 4 – 6

300 g/11 oz canned apricot halves in fruit juice

1 x 5 ml spoon/1 teaspoon arrowroot

toasted flaked almonds

PASTRY

100 g/4 oz plain flour

a pinch of salt

50 g/2 oz butter

50 g/2 oz caster *or* icing sugar

1 egg, beaten

FILLING

300 ml/½ pint milk

25 g/1 oz caster sugar

25 g/1 oz cornflour

2 egg yolks

½ x 2.5 ml spoon/¼ teaspoon almond essence

Pat's Apricot and Almond Tart

Make the pastry first. Sift the flour and salt into a basin. Make a well in the centre and add the butter, sugar and egg. Work the ingredients together, adding a little cold water, if necessary, until a soft dough is formed. Roll out on a lightly floured surface and use to line a 20 cm/8 inch French fluted flan tin. Chill for 30 minutes, then prick the base and bake blind in a fairly hot oven, 190°C/375°F/Gas 5, for 20 – 25 minutes until golden. Leave to cool, then remove from the tin.

Meanwhile, prepare the filling. Heat the milk and sugar in a saucepan. Mix together the cornflour and egg yolks, then pour the milk over the mixture. Stir well, then strain back into the pan. Cook over gentle heat, stirring constantly until thickened. Off the heat, stir in the almond essence. Leave to cool, then spread over the base of the baked pastry case.

Drain the apricots, reserving the juice, and arrange the apricots on the custard. Stir the arrowroot into the reserved apricot juice, and bring to the boil, stirring until thickened. Cool slightly, then brush over the apricots to glaze them. Scatter with the almonds.

MY PLUMS WITH PORT

Serves 6

900 g/2 lb plums

100 – 175 g/4 – 6 oz soft light brown sugar

150 ml/¼ pint port

Cut the plums neatly in half and remove the stones. Put the fruit into a baking dish or casserole, sprinkle with the sugar (the amount required will depend on the sweetness of the plums) and pour the port on top. Cover securely with a lid or foil and bake in a cool oven, 150°C/300°F/Gas 2, for 45 – 60 minutes or until the plums are tender. Serve hot, or lightly chilled.

DOLLY'S CHOCOLATE PROFITEROLES

Serves 8

CHOUX PASTRY

300 ml/¹/₂ pint water
50 g/2 oz butter *or* margarine
a pinch of salt
100 g/4 oz plain flour, sifted
1 egg yolk
2 eggs

CHANTILLY CREAM

300 ml/¹/₂ pint double cream, chilled for several hours
25 g/1 oz caster sugar
vanilla essence

CHOCOLATE GLACÉ ICING

100 g/4 oz plain chocolate, grated
2 x 15 ml spoons/2 tablespoons water
4 x 5 ml spoons/4 teaspoons softened butter
225 g/8 oz icing sugar, sifted

Prepare the choux pastry first. Put the water, fat and salt in a saucepan, and bring to the boil. Remove from the heat and add the flour all at once. Return to the heat and beat well with a wooden spoon until the mixture forms a smooth paste which leaves the sides of the pan clean. Remove from the heat, cool slightly, add the egg yolk, and beat well. Add the other eggs, one at a time, beating thoroughly between each addition.

Put the mixture in a forcing bag with a 2.5 cm/ 1 inch nozzle and pipe 24 – 30 small choux on to a lightly greased baking sheet. Bake in a hot oven, 220°C/425°F/Gas 7, for 30 minutes. Reduce the heat to moderate, 180°C/350°F/Gas 4, and bake for a further 10 minutes. Remove the choux from the oven, open them at the bottom, remove any uncooked paste, and leave to dry out and cool completely.

Meanwhile, whip the cream lightly. Just before using, whip in the sugar and a few drops of vanilla essence to taste.

To prepare the glacé icing, gently warm the chocolate, water and butter in a small pan, stirring constantly until the mixture is smooth and creamy.

Stir in the icing sugar, a little at a time, adding a little extra water if necessary to make a coating consistency.

Fill the cold choux buns with the Chantilly cream, and glaze the tops with the glacé icing, reserving some for assembling the dish. Let the icing harden, then arrange the choux in a pyramid – this is easiest done if they can be arranged against the sides of a conical mould. Stick them together with small dabs of reserved icing. Serve three or four choux per person, with hot Chocolate Sauce.

CHOCOLATE SAUCE

Makes 175 ml/6 fl oz (approx)

100 g/4 oz plain chocolate, broken into pieces
225 g/8 oz sugar
150 ml/¹/₄ pint black coffee
salt
1 x 2.5 ml spoon/¹/₂ teaspoon vanilla essence

Put the chocolate into a saucepan with the other ingredients and stir over gentle heat until the chocolate and sugar melt and blend together. Serve hot over profiteroles.

Dolly's Chocolate Profiteroles

ABOVE Dolly's Chocolate Mousse

RIGHT Pat's Fruit Salad Basket

PAT'S FRUIT SALAD BASKET

Serves 4

675 g/1½ lb mixed fresh and dried fruit
prepared and sliced, cubed etc as required

1 melon

FRUIT SYRUP

pared rind and juice of 1 lemon

600 ml/1 pint water

75 g/3 oz sugar

brandy

Make the fruit syrup first. Put the lemon rind and
juice into a pan with the water and sugar. Heat
gently until the sugar has dissolved, then bring to
the boil, and continue boiling until the syrup has
been reduced by about half. Flavour with brandy,
then remove from the heat, strain and cool.
Put the mixed fruit into the syrup as soon as it
has been prepared, mix together and leave for
2 – 3 hours to allow the flavours to blend.
To make the melon basket, cut two equal-sized
wedges from either side of the top half of the melon,
leaving a 2.5 cm/1 inch piece intact for the handle.
Carefully cut out the flesh from the handle, leaving
a 1.25 cm/½ inch rim. Scoop out the flesh from the
lower section and add to the fruit salad. Fill the
melon with the prepared fruit, and serve on a bed
of crushed ice.

DOLLY'S CHOCOLATE MOUSSE

Serves 4

175 g/6 oz plain chocolate, broken up

2 x 15 ml spoons/2 tablespoons water

4 eggs, separated

vanilla essence

DECORATION

whipped double cream

chopped nuts

Put the chocolate into a large heatproof basin with
the water and stand over a pan of hot water. Heat
gently until the chocolate melts. Remove from the
heat and stir until smooth. Beat the yolks and a few
drops of vanilla essence into the chocolate. Whisk
the egg whites until fairly stiff, and fold gently into
the mixture until evenly blended. Pour into four
individual dishes and leave for 1 – 2 hours to set.
Serve decorated with cream and chopped nuts.

Index

125